Our mission is to celebrate the art, skill, and heritage of quilting and fiber arts, while enhancing the cultural vitality of Sisters and Central Oregon and providing enrichment opportunities for area youth.

**SISTERS OUTDOOR QUILT SHOW
MISSION STATEMENT**

Sisters, Oregon
Five Decades of Quilting in America

SISTERS, OREGON

Five Decades of Quilting in America

JEAN WELLS

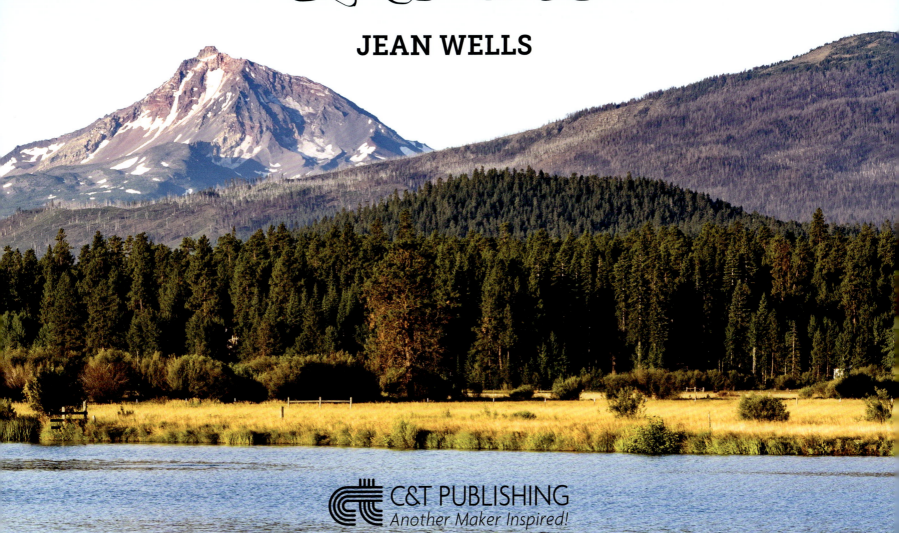

C&T PUBLISHING
Another Maker Inspired!

Text copyright © 2025 by Jean Ann Wells Keenan

Photography copyright © 2025 by Jean Ann Wells Keenan

Artwork copyright © 2025 by C&T Publishing

PUBLISHER: Amy Barrett-Daffin

CREATIVE DIRECTOR: Gailen Runge

SENIOR EDITOR: Roxane Cerda

ASSOCIATE EDITOR: Karly Wallace

COPY EDITOR: Elizabeth Kuball of Nordvest LLC

COVER/BOOK DESIGNER: April Mostek

PRODUCTION COORDINATOR: Zinnia Heinzmann

ILLUSTRATOR: Ginn Staines

PHOTOGRAPHY COORDINATOR: Rachel Ackley

FRONT COVER PHOTOGRAPHY by Valori Wells

TITLE PAGE PHOTOGRAPHY by Bob Pool/Shutterstock.com

PHOTOGRAPHY by Olivia Kennedy and Valori Wells, unless otherwise noted

Published by C&T Publishing, Inc., P.O. Box 1456, Lafayette, CA 94549

All rights reserved. No part of this work covered by the copyright hereon may be used in any form or reproduced by any means—graphic, electronic, or mechanical, including photocopying, recording, taping, or information storage and retrieval systems—without written permission from the publisher. The copyrights on individual artworks are retained by the artists as noted in *Sisters, Oregon—Five Decades of Quilting in America*. These designs may be used to make items for personal use only and may not be used for the purpose of personal profit. Items created to benefit nonprofit groups, or that will be publicly displayed, must be conspicuously labeled with the following credit: "Designs copyright © 2025 by Jean Wells from the book *Sisters, Oregon—Five Decades of Quilting in America* from C&T Publishing, Inc." Permission for all other purposes must be requested in writing from C&T Publishing, Inc.

Attention Teachers: C&T Publishing, Inc., encourages the use of our books as texts for teaching. You can find lesson plans for many of our titles at ctpub.com or contact us at ctinfo@ctpub.com.

We take great care to ensure that the information included in our products is accurate and presented in good faith, but no warranty is provided, nor are results guaranteed. Having no control over the choices of materials or procedures used, neither the author nor C&T Publishing, Inc., shall have any liability to any person or entity with respect to any loss or damage caused directly or indirectly by the information contained in this book. For your convenience, we post an up-to-date listing of corrections on our website (ctpub.com). If a correction is not already noted, please contact our customer service department at ctinfo@ctpub.com or P.O. Box 1456, Lafayette, CA 94549.

Trademark (™) and registered trademark (®) names are used throughout this book. Rather than use the symbols with every occurrence of a trademark or registered trademark name, we are using the names only in the editorial fashion and to the benefit of the owner, with no intention of infringement.

Library of Congress Cataloging-in-Publication Data

Names: Wells, Jean, author.

Title: Sisters, Oregon--five decades of quilting in America / by Jean Wells.

Description: Lafayette, CA : C&T Publishing, [2025] | Summary: "Go behind the scenes of the world's largest outdoor quilt show and celebrate the community of quilters that comes together every year in a small Oregon town. Learn how quilter Jean Wells, her family, the art of quilting, and a small community nestled at the foot of gorgeous mountains intertwined to grow together and flourish"-- Provided by publisher.

Identifiers: LCCN 2024057553 | ISBN 9781644035467 (hardcover) | ISBN 9781644035474 (ebook)

Subjects: LCSH: Sisters Outdoor Quilt Show--History | Patchwork quilts--Oregon--Sisters--Exhibitions--History. | Art quilts--Oregon--Sisters--Exhibitions--History.

Classification: LCC TT835 .W46555 2025 | DDC 746.4609795--dc23/eng/20250124

LC record available at https://lccn.loc.gov/2024057553

Printed in China

10 9 8 7 6 5 4 3 2 1

Front cover quilts left to right: Rescued velvet Log Cabin quilt-as-you-go quilt; *Grace Log Cabin* in the round quilt by Valori and Jean Wells; *Fireworks* by Donna Kozel, begun in a Quilter's Affair workshop.

dedication

I want to honor my family members who pitch in for setup and takedown, picking up teachers from the airport, helping in the Stitchin' Post, working at Quilter's Affair, and acting as ambassadors to the quilt show attendees. I am immensely proud that all five of my grandchildren have made a quilt and entered it into the show.

I am so grateful to my daughter, Valori for taking over the operations of the store and the leadership of Quilter's Affair. I am really enjoying seeing the changes she is making. My son, Jason, and his wife Maggie always seem to be in the right place at the right time and have taken over many of my responsibilities. My sister, June Jaeger, was a huge support while writing this book as well as volunteering tirelessly for the quilt show. John, my dear husband, is always there for me. Every morning of our married years he has asked me if there is anything he can do for me that day. During the busy days of preparation, he has a big list and usually finds me someplace that day with a glass of my favorite iced tea.

On the day of the quilt show, around 10 o'clock, once our chores are done, we all come together and walk through town, admiring the beautiful quilts, pointing out our favorites. This past summer my 21-year-old grandson purchased a quilt for himself at the show. My oldest granddaughter took many of the photos you will see in this book, while the others helped out at the Stitchin' Post. It truly is a family affair.

Contents

Foreword, 8

Introduction, 10

The First Years, 14
- *The Love Affair, 16*
- *The Stitchin' Post, 17*
- *The First Show, 20*
- *The Early Years: 1976–1979, 22*
- *Blossoming: 1980–1989, 27*

Finding Fertile Ground, 36
- *The Locals, 38*
- *Flourishing, 40*
- *A New Home, 44*
- *The 25th Anniversary, 51*

Becoming Today's Show, 54
- *The Tipping Point, 56*
- *Fresh Features, 60*
- *New Horizons, 71*
- *When Plans Change, 83*

Community, 94
- *The Businesses, 97*
- *Drawn into the Art, 105*
- *The Volunteers, 109*
- *The Quilt Show Gives Back, 114*

The Quilts, 116

The Educators, 130

Local Artists, 150

The Show Today, 164
- *Save It for Sunday, 170*

The Sisters Outdoor Quilt Show Posters, 178

Photography Credits, 187

About the Author, 189

About the Contributors 190

Foreword

By Tula Pink

When I first tried to write this foreword for a book about the life and quilting contributions of Jean Wells, I struggled to find the right words. After some introspection, I discovered the glaring flaw in my approach. Initially, I attempted to write from the perspective of Jean's equal but this is not how I view her. To write this honestly I had to write from the perspective of looking up, not eye to eye. Simply put, Jean is a legend. She is an accomplished artist, a quilting visionary, a successful businesswoman, a nurturer of talent in others, a builder of communities, a brilliant educator, and a person I feel so lucky to call a friend.

Jean has always been a giant in this industry. I first came to know her through her work. I stumbled across one of her books *Intuitive Color and Design* a few years after I entered the business of quilting. Her approach to line, shape, and color was so fresh and new to me. It always struck me as like a haiku in patchwork. A structure and method underpinned the whole thing but the overall effect was like a breath released at a specific moment in time. While I am sure the works were labored over they always gave me the impression that they appeared fully formed; like a snapshot of the natural world that our human eyes are not sophisticated enough to capture before it dissipates into mist. The improvisational nature of her work implies a mind that is flexible, ever-changing, and adapting, a mind in constant motion. I was a fan of Jean Wells as an artist before I ever had the pleasure of meeting her.

Once in a great while you meet a person with a sort of quiet kind of power. This person will say what they mean and mean what they say. It is surprising how rare that is. When I first met Jean in person I was a fledgling fabric designer with a couple of collections under my belt. I loved what I was doing but was still not sure that anyone else would agree. Jean was one of the first people to tell me that my work was valuable. She said it directly and with the confidence that only someone who had seen thousands of fabrics and designers come and go over the years could master. I believed her earnestness and continued on. That little bit of encouragement from someone I respected would get me through those early salad days and stay with me long after others began to take notice. It is easy to see the flaws in things but to truly see the potential in people and encourage those coming up and still finding their way has an impact that can last forever. Jean has that kind of impact on myself and countless others. Her generosity of spirit is something that I hope to live up to in my own career. I believe it is this quality that makes her such an extraordinary teacher.

Teaching is about giving all of yourself to your students. To do it well you have to leave your ego at the door and meet each and every student where they are. Jean has given a small piece of herself and her talent to every student she has ever taught. I initially took her classes to learn how to be a better teacher. I left being a better artist. She doesn't dictate or make demands of her students. She doesn't push her students to work like her. She guides her students to their own creative intuition and helps them find a voice of their own. Jean identifies the magic hidden within each student and guides them to unlock their own resources as a true teacher does.

The community that Jean has built around the Sisters Outdoor Quilt Show and the preceding week of education is unlike anything that I have ever attended anywhere in the world. To create a special event once is a feat unto itself. To create an event that keeps going and growing for 50 years would be unimaginable if I did not have the pleasure of experiencing it myself over these last 15 years. I wasn't there for its origins but what it has become is one of the most special events surrounding the quilting year. The respect and integrity that embodies this event between the teachers, students, and staff is something that must come from the top. It cannot be manufactured. As we all descend upon Sisters, Oregon, every year we feel like we

are coming home. It is a magical week filled with friends, people, camaraderie, shared passions, and of course a lot of quilts! Teaching can often feel like a job but this feels like service not just to the students but for our own souls. We leave fuller than when we arrived and that is because of Jean's spirit and the foundations she laid down 50 years ago.

Thank you, Jean, from the bottom of my heart for everything that you have given me, the quilting community, and the legacy that you have left in your illustrious wake. May we all live up to your beautiful example!

LEFT (2) • *Tula's quilts displayed at the 2015 Save It for Sunday! show.*

RIGHT • *Tula, teaching at Quilter's Affair.*

Foreword

Introduction

Loving fabric and wanting to sew as a little girl, I would have never thought that I would grow up to write Sisters, Oregon—Five Decades of Quilting in America! As a young mother and self-taught quilter, I never imagined I would end up traveling the globe sharing my love of quilting and writing dozens of books. I had grown to love teaching and wanted a place to teach. The foundation of The Stitchin' Post was *Inspiration and Education* and it remains that way today.

In 1975, when the opportunity for my new friend and fellow shop owner and I to hold a summer festival I hung a dozen quilts outdoors and the largest Outdoor Quilt Show in America was born. With remarkable synergy, quilting itself grew right alongside my quilting knowledge and the show, going from what had almost become a lost art to the flourishing industry and community that it is today. From the very beginning, the community of Sisters and the community of quilters supported us just as we support our hometown and the larger quilting community from first-time quiltmakers to veteran instructors who come to town to share their knowledge.

Quilting is multi-faceted in Sisters, Oregon. Year-round, The Stitchin' Post offers education, inspiration, and supplies to quilters of all types, both near and far. The week before our Quilt Show, the Quilter's Affair welcomes 1,200 students and 30 instructors to come to our small town and learn from one another. And, the second Saturday in July, the Sisters Outdoor Quilt Show welcomes thousands of folks to join in the celebration of the creative quilting experience.

Online and in person The Stitchin' Post embraces quilters and creates community with unique, exclusive products, free educational videos, and classes ranging from Beginning Boot Camp Quilting to intensive five-day workshops given by nationally-recognized instructors. Expanding upon our love of sharing and inspirational making, we also offer our customers the opportunity to explore knitting and other fiber arts.

You are invited to join us in this wonderful world of quilting in the community of Sisters, Oregon. I hope you get to experience a bit of the magic for yourself.

Jean

LEFT • The Stitchin' Post caters to not just quilters of all types, but also offers inspiration for knitters and other fiber artists.

TOP • The Stitchin' Post, adorned with quilts and welcoming visitors on Quilt Show day.

 "From a tiny spark of an idea in 1975, in a tiny community in Central Oregon, Sisters Outdoor Quilt Show has become a powerful engine that moves an entire industry, namely the textile arts, and the village of Sisters itself. Over the past 50 years, generations of quilters have been inspired by the wild, whimsical, wonderful annual event. Tens of thousands of people have been drawn to the Show, contributing millions of dollars to the local economy. Throughout, the Show has stayed relevant and on trend, a leader in the quilting world, and is a bucket list for textile artists and admirers worldwide."—Jan McGowan, former member of the board of directors, Sisters Outdoor Quilt Show

TOP • Some of my quilts hung at the FivePine Lodge & Conference Center the day after the show for our Save It for Sunday! event.

RIGHT • My son Jason and grandson Braden hanging a quilt in the Teacher's Pavillion early on Quilt Show morning.

the First Years

Two early shop samplers.

The appliqué quilt made for the nursery of my first child, Jason.

The Love Affair

In the spring of 1969, as an expectant young mother, I decided to take an appliqué workshop with Jean Ray Laury. That little spark, coupled with stumbling upon a photograph of a Log Cabin pillow in *Family Circle* magazine, kindled a lifelong love affair with patchwork.

The Log Cabin block intrigued me, and I puzzled over how it was constructed. One day, it dawned on me that I needed to begin with a square and then add strips of fabric to each side. I felt like I'd discovered something truly wonderful! Already a full-time home economics teacher, I started teaching patchwork and quilting classes to adults at the community college. These arts had long been asleep in America, but bit by bit, they were awakening.

Debbie Newport, school counselor and lifelong Sisters citizen, recalls that, in 1972, about the same time quilting was beginning to reawaken, Brooks Resources in Bend, Oregon, opened Black Butte Ranch, its new development west of Sisters. "At the same time, they invested in the town of Sisters, supporting the growth of businesses that provided 'supplies' for residents and visitors to BBR—groceries, building supplies, hardware, etc.—and the first little 'tourist shops' that encouraged strolling through the town. The ranch funded upgrades to storefronts in town, helping create an 1880s western theme, and move the small logging town in a new direction.

"The population of Sisters increased, businesses popped up, and activities to attract vacationers were bringing new interest to this little town on the east slope of the Three Sisters mountains. What had become a dwindling logging and timber town was being reinvented."

The Stitchin' Post

Little did I know that, when I discovered that Log Cabin pillow on the *Family Circle* magazine cover, I'd soon cash in my retirement account and use the $3,500 to buy goods for my very own fabric store. As a career teacher, I knew from the beginning that I wanted a space where I could both teach classes and offer supplies to students.

My 92-year-old grandmother, Meda Butler, who taught me to sew, came out from Redmond, Oregon, to visit the store. Grandma Meda was an expert seamstress and made beautiful garments for my sisters and me, as well as our dolls. Widowed as a young woman, she continued to run the drugstore her husband had started in the neighboring town of Redmond. When she walked in the door, she exclaimed, 'I had a pharmacy in this very room in the 1930s!' I was thrilled to have this connection with my grandma.

TOP • My first Log Cabin quilt.

BOTTOM • The original storefront and sign.

The original Stitchin' Post logo, design by Cathi Howell.

I carried my passion for teaching into the shop. *Inspiration and Education* was the shop's mission, and when I opened the doors to the Stitchin' Post, I reserved a 10′ × 14′ space in the store where I could teach classes. From the beginning, the shop has been supported by community. My then-new friend and boutique owner, Cathi Howell, created the artwork for my sign. Carrol Clark, my best friend from college, created the first shop flier. Together they helped organize the shop opening.

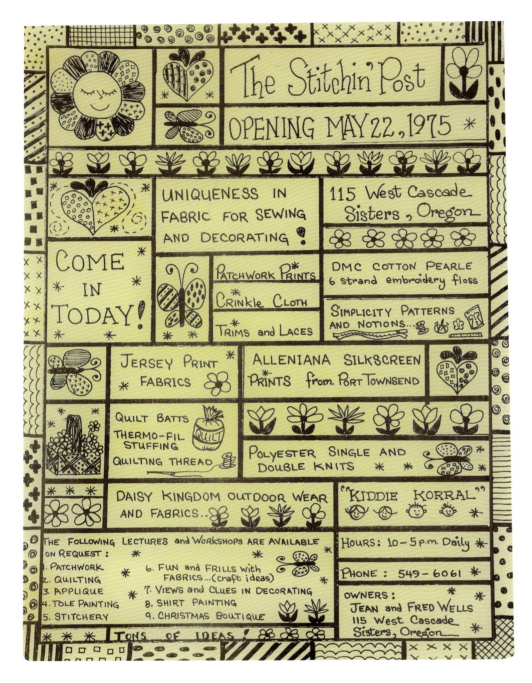

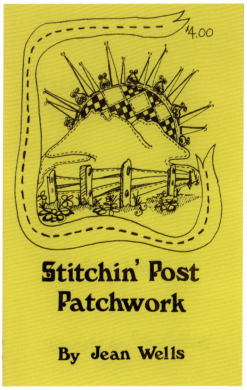

LEFT • The first Stitchin' Post flyer.

RIGHT (2) • Using the skills I had gained teaching home economics, I created a small booklet, *Stitchin' Post Patchwork* to use as a class resource and a *Puff Patchwork Purse* pattern.

The First Show

Cathi Howell suggested having a craft fair one Saturday in July. She would display some of her pottery and handmade accessories outside, and I could hang some quilts. At this time in my life, I'd only made quilts for my children, Jason and Valori, and those were well worn. I knew my mother stored family quilts in the cedar chest at her house in Redmond, so I borrowed them to hang alongside a couple of Cathi's family quilts. My ancestors came to Oregon on the Oregon Trail, which makes me a fifth-generation Oregonian on my grandmother's side. As I drove away from my mother's house with the car full of quilts to hang in the quilt show, I reminisced about playing under the quilting frame as a little girl at my grandmother Lotta Morse's house. Now, here I was sharing family quilts made by her on that same frame. All in all, we hung twelve quilts that first year.

Cathi remembers that "In the early 1970s, I moved to Sisters to open a small shop that sold consignment arts and crafts—pottery, some antiques, jewelry, quilts and a plethora of other 'crafty' items.

"As I recall, one afternoon, Jean and her two small children came into the shop, which I had named the Cubbyhole. She told me that she and her family were moving to the area.

"Not long after that initial meeting, Jean started teaching patchwork and quilting for the community college, and subsequent to that, she opened the first Stitchin' Post shop ... so aptly named as Sisters was wanting to conform to a western theme as a tourist destination.

"The Stitchin' Post was located in a space in the old Hotel Sisters. Not long after Jean moved in, I decided to expand and move into a newer space in the recently built Barclay Square. Jean and I were almost neighbors.

LEFT • Me, hanging quilts for our very first show.

MIDDLE • Cathi (left) and Jean (right).

RIGHT • The first Quilt Show.

"It was an exciting time in Sisters ... new ideas and small businesses giving it a try. Jean and I talked about creating events that would emphasize the western theme and bring business to town and give attention to our crafty stores.

"The first annual quilt show was one of those ideas ... combined with a few other art/craft displays. It also coincided with the 75th birthday of Sisters!

"Most of the first twelve quilts on display were Jean's family pieces. I recall a couple of my grandma's quilts in the mix there as well.

"And so it began!"

The most wonderful thing happened that Saturday as people from Sisters came to see what we were up to. They asked if they could bring quilts to hang, too. From the very beginning, the show became a day of sharing. The magic that happened that day in July 1975 still exists today as the Sisters Outdoor Quilt Show, which has grown to a show of more than 1,000 quilts.

"By 1975 The Sisters Rodeo had become a mainstay attraction, and the Sisters Outdoor Quilt Show sprang out of the walls of a tiny little fabric shop on the main street of town, quickly becoming an annual event that continues to attract people from across the country and beyond," Debbie Newport shares.

The Early Years: 1976–1979

My sister, June Jaeger, recalls that the next year, 1976, several quilters in Sisters also wanted to hang their quilts in the show, and she contributed several of her own antique quilts to hang alongside. "They lined both sides of Cascade Avenue. The business owners would come out and visit with the viewers, and word quickly got around that we should do this every year. In a few years, Sisters Outdoors Quilt Show, also known as Jean's Quilt Show, had grown, with quilts hanging from balconies, buildings and between trees. The shop owners volunteered to help hang quilts, as well as people attending the show. Word got around, and folks were coming from greater Oregon to see the show. All styles of quilts were welcome in the show. There was no jurying. You would see a quilter's first quilt, as well as antique quilts hanging side by side."

With the popularity of the show growing, I developed an information sheet for the entrant to fill out and found a place in Bend, Oregon, that printed up participant ribbons for us to hang on each of the quilts. From then on, everyone went home with a ribbon. I also asked each entrant to fill out information on a recipe card, which I kept in a box. I began to sort through the quilts, looking for something they had in common with their neighbor, to plan how they would be displayed. It might be color, the block design, or content if it was a pictorial quilt. It was a joyful process to see all of the work that went in the quilts up close and to showcase them the very best that I could.

Red and white was the theme for this corner.

Spring '77 Fabric Market

$1.20

the newspaper for the ready-to-sew market

Fabricnews

New York   Los Angeles

September, 1976

Vol. 7 Special Issue

In Oregon
Smaller Is Better

SISTERS, ORE.--Scorning the bigger-is-better trend that's produced yardage barns and defunct supermarkets-turned-fabric stores, Jean Wells designed a tiny, personalized sewing shop "with the Western woman in mind." Fifteen months ago she opened The Stitchin' Post, country-style and probably one-of-a-kind not only in this resort town of 600, but in the nation as well.

Instead of fabric tables, Ms. Wells displays bolts on brass beds and in restored trunks. Antique Coca-Cola bottle boxes are decoupaged and hold thread spools. "Growing" in wooden flower boxes are trims and notions. Customers find remnants in heirloom chest of drawers. Ms. Wells' favorite plants thrive among the fabrics and homespun furnishings in the sunshine yellow shop. All of this on The Stitchin' Post's meager plot – 14' by 40' in a rustic Sisters' hotel.

Jean Wells moved to Sisters from Portland where she taught home economics – and sewing classes at Daisy Kingdom, a make-your-own skiwear specialist. Wanting a "completely different" fabric store, she transformed the location with hand-me-down fixtures, yellow paint and not more than $50, into "The Stitchin' Post". Ms. Wells knew the merchandise had to be in keeping with the hand-crafted look so she spent her first $3,500 on calico prints, basic checks and dots, plus a few basics – all cotton wovens for the prairie-look projects she displays on walls, in windows, and from the 20 ft. ceilings. Ms. Wells believed what she liked would sell.

Stitchin' Posts' Jean Wells: "It looks like fun and it is, but it's been hard work too."

Evidently her personalized buying approach works. Monthly volume continues to double and her initial $3,500 inventory has grown to $16,000. She proudly points to four fabric turns in seven months. Now added to the ever popular calicos are Pacific Northwest-inspired silk screen prints perfect for change library. "When a pattern style is popular, there's no reason for it not to be re-used by another customer."

To promote sewing and the Stitchin' Post, she teaches classes, from skiwear to Christmas craft items, at a more spacious neighboring school. Classes fill quickly for

In Texas
A Fashion Trade-Up

DALLAS, TEXAS--Yes, Virginia, there is a high fashion fabric shop that attracts the wealthiest people in a city of wealthy people. They're attracted by the custom fashion available there and by the carefully honed elite atmosphere — Richard Brooks is a Tiffany of fabric stores in this Southwestern metropolis which also spawned Neiman-Marcus and $100,000 Christmas gift suggestions.

believes that the market is geared for retailers who haven't been trained in fashion. "They assume fabric retailers are dumb." Pointing to the last AHSC fashion show, Brooks comments "I didn't learn anything. The garments looked terrible and the fabrics looked sleazy."

Majoring in fashion merchandising at Louisiana State University, Brooks became intrigued by fabric rather than ready-to-wear retailing.

Brooks regards his "fashion homework" all-important and cites the designer ready-to-wear market as his primary source of information. He won't be "told" what's fashion. "Let's take for example UltraSuede. We do a tremendous business with that but those new prints they've put on it are just plain awful. Skinner should have taken the responsibility of to keep those out of the market."

"Smaller is Better SISTERS, ORE.—Scorning the bigger-is-better trend that's produced yardage barns and defunct supermarkets-turned-fabric stores, Jean Wells designed a tiny, personalized sewing shop "with the western woman in mind." Fifteen months ago, she opened the Stitchin' Post, country-style and probably one-of-a-kind not only in this resort town of 600, but in the nation as well." "Smaller is Better." Fabricnews, September 1976.

23

The First Years

"It is truly amazing that we are remembering back 50 years to the very first Sisters Outdoor Quilt Show. I remember the funky little building on the west end of town that Jean first hung her family quilts on. It was charming and welcoming from the very beginning.

"I feel so fortunate to have been able to experience and participate in the Quilt Show over so many years. I didn't learn to quilt until 1992, but I did sew, knit, and embroider. I loved following the Stitchin' Post as it moved around town in the early days before settling in their lovely current location.

"At the urging of my niece, we signed up for the very first Jean Wells sampler classes. I was hooked immediately! It literally changed my life. I do credit my dear friend, Jean, for the inspiration, encouragement, and creativity that has kept all of us drenched in color, design, and camaraderie for 50-plus years. It is an honor and a privilege to be a part of such a successful and inclusive event as the Sisters Outdoor Quilt Show."—Tonye B. Phillips, instructor and author.

TOP • Dozens of quilts hung for all to enjoy.

BOTTOM • Dede Gilchrist (left) and Barbara Slater (right) discuss their love of quilting.

Over time the businesses changed, but each year they were all bedecked in quilts.

In 1978, a few years into the show, I had the idea to bring in a popular quilter to give a lecture the day before the show. Mary Ellen Hopkins, a well-known author and lecturer, was very entertaining, and quilters from all around Central Oregon came to hear her speak. The next year, I added three workshops, and in 1980, the popular educational event officially became the Quilter's Affair, and the Stitchin' Post is responsible for the event to this day. In 2025, it will boast 30 instructors and offer five days of workshops and lectures during the week leading up to the show.

Four years into the show, seven ladies from Sisters formed an informal quilt guild. East of the Cascades Quilters was led by Elizabeth Duncan, a retired teacher, genealogist, writer, historian, and quilter. The guild's main focus was to help put on the show every year on the second Saturday of July and to explore quiltmaking. Our community of quilters was coming together.

In 1980, I was invited to teach a workshop at the first West Coast Quilter's Conference held in Portland, Oregon. After seeing my handouts and patchwork garments, Marti Michell, from the publishing house Yours Truly, invited me to write a book on patchwork clothing, kicking off my professional writing career.

"The number of quilts hung soon reached 100, which felt huge for these seven women. The show had become a festival, a reunion, and an event on people's bucket list, giving the small town of Sisters its place on the map," remembers June Jaeger.

The First Years

In the early years, we tried a number of new things. To celebrate the fourth show, Joyce Coats, a devoted customer from Bend, and I came up with the idea of making and decorating sheet cakes to resemble quilt blocks. On the day before the show, Joyce and I, along with two of Joyce's daughters, gathered at my house to decorate the cakes. On the morning of the show, my husband removed the mattress from my daughter Valori's bed, and reassembled it in town. He put a plywood sheet across the frame and we arranged all of the sheet cakes on it.

Valori, six at the time, wore one of her patchwork dresses to greet visitors as folks sampled the quilt cake.

Blossoming: 1980–1989

The world of quilting was developing apace with our small-but-growing quilt show. According to quilting instructor Lawry Thorn, "When the rotary cutter came into our lives, there was no more cutting out templates and cutting fabric with scissors. Mary Ellen Hopkins developed 'Perfect Piecing' workshops and Ginn Staines, a resident of Sisters and I attended; then we came back to the shop and taught classes. At one of the workshops, Harriet Hargrave introduced machine quilting on her domestic sewing machine. It became very popular. Hand quilting almost became a thing of the past."

"Little did I know when my husband, daughter, and I moved here and I found the Stitchin' Post inside the Hotel Sisters building what an influence Jean would have on me," recalls Lawry Thorn, Stitchin' Post employee and instructor. *After the shop moved to a new building on Elm Street, Lawry stopped in. During her visit she found that I needed someone to work in the shop an afternoon or two a week. The rest, as Lawry recalls, is history "I volunteered, and so many opportunities opened up for me …. These started with working the shop, [led] to managing the shop, and then being bookkeeper, to sending me to seminars and teaching classes, traveling to Quilt Market [the annual quilt industry trade show in Houston, Texas], … helping with Quilt Show, plus showing my quilts in almost every show for many years. I have [also] been honored as Featured Quilter and … was selected to be the first Inspirational Instructor."*

Jason and Valori turned out in my patchwork garments.

The show and patchwork were not the only things experiencing a revitalization. Beverly Thacker, Registered Economic Development Specialist for the State of Oregon, notes, "In the 1980s and '90s, when Oregon's timber-based economy collapsed, communities whose economies were dependent on a steady supply of cheap federal timber, were forced to reinvent themselves. Tourism was seen as an obvious solution.

"Local, regional, and state economic development professionals looked to Sisters's success as a model. This small timber town was booming in the midst of an economic downturn—all due to the efforts of a few farsighted individuals who had 'branded' their town and were attracting tourists with a main street featuring stores with western-style false fronts, enterprises called the Stitchin' Post, the Sisters Saloon, a community newspaper called *The Nugget*, etc., selling antiques, food, drink, and atmosphere. Not to mention events like the Sisters Rodeo and the soon-to-become-world-famous annual Sisters Outdoor Quilt Show.

"Everyone wanted to become the next Sisters."

1981 saw the publication of my first book, *Patchworthy Apparel*, illustrated by talented local artist and young mother Marina Wood. My publisher sent a copy of the book to *Good Housekeeping* magazine. Cecilia Toth, an editor with the magazine, hired me to create mother/daughter strip-pieced garments for a four-page spread in their Needlecraft issue.

Interest in patchwork was continuing to grow across the country, and this same year, I was invited to teach workshops at the annual International Quilt Show in Houston, Texas. I would later end up teaching patchwork and business classes to fellow shop owners for years, and I continued to teach until 2012. During these early sessions, I came up with the idea of cutting up fabric into smaller pieces to sell; the very first fat quarter (an 18″ × 22″ rectangle of fabric). That particular cut is still popular today. The Stitchin' Post has always been a trendsetter, and even in the early days we brought in popular quilting instructors to come and teach workshops. Following the Stitchin' Post's example, I was one of the early quilters hired by quilt guilds to travel to lecture and give workshops, the first of which was to a Milwaukee, Wisconsin, quilt guild. Quilters were beginning to share tastes and techniques across the country.

The Only Awards

Though the show itself has never given awards, we launched the first annual Quilt Block Contest in 1981, as an exhibit at the show. The contest theme was pine trees, and it was open to members of the East of the Cascades Guild. The contest continued for several years with different themes and judging by Quilt Show attendees. In the early '80s, Jennifer Sampou and I created Pine Brook, a line of fabric that was featured in one of the first Quilt Block Contests.

As the prize, one of the makers of the blocks wins all of the blocks. Then, if they like, they can put them together in a quilt. The quilt below was created by Margaret Peters, who won the Pine Brook quilt blocks that year.

As recalled by quilt artist Janet M. Tetzlaff, "By 1985, the contest was opened to non-guild members, but the requirement was added to use fabric chosen by SOQS and donated by a sponsoring fabric company. Quilter's Affair teachers began judging the blocks in 2001, awarding a cash prize, ribbons, and fabric to first- through third-place winners.

"In recent years, more than 50 quiltmakers have joined the Quilt Block Contest and submitted blocks to be judged, part of a tradition almost as old as the Quilt Show itself."

The current executive director, Dawn M. Boyd, notes that the "blocks entered include a variety of quilting styles, reflecting the multitude of artists who participate. Traditional pieced blocks, applique and collage blocks, plus embellishments reveal each participant's personality and artistry."

Steppin' Out *by Jean Wells (left) and Pine Brook quilt by Margaret Peters (right).*

An early quilt block contest, sponsored by Westminster Fibers.

The First Years

By 1982, the show's seventh year, it had grown to more than 200 quilts entered, which required a formal registration process, which at the time felt huge. That year, we hosted four instructors for the Quilter's Affair and the East of the Cascades Quilters created the first raffle quilt to raise funds to offset operational costs of the show. Just like the town itself, the show was getting traction.

Though many show events developed into annual features, according to Ginn Staines, Sisters, Oregon, resident, "The first and final 5K Sisters Outdoor Quilt Show Run took place at 8:00 a.m., Saturday, July 10, 1982. Fifty participants started in the area east of the Sisters Fire Hall, ran through the pine forest along Three Creeks Road, and ended up in downtown Sisters. Prizes and a raffle followed. A good time was had by all."

In 1983, I was divorced and realized that in order to support myself and my two children and continue to live in Sisters, I needed to learn how to be a better businesswoman. I enrolled in a three-year small business management program at Central Oregon Community College. I embraced the program, thanks to my advisor, Reese Shephard.

The small business management program gave me knowledge that I later was able to share with other quilt shop owners at Quilt Market, the annual quilt industry trade show in Houston, Texas. By better understanding how to use the information in monthly profit-and-loss statements and balance sheets, I found joy in the business side of owning a business. My advisor had me complete an extensive customer survey, and I realized that only 35 percent of my customers were from Sisters and greater Central Oregon; the rest came from outside the area. At that time, I was spending all of my advertising dollars locally, which soon changed.

I shared what I was learning with other businesses in Sisters, and many of those business owners, in turn, enrolled in the program. The program was such a great fit for me that I became something of a poster child for the program and was quoted for years to come in their advertising.

The first raffle quilt, made by the East of the Cascades Quilters, featured the classic Pine Tree block.

Through the program, I had the opportunity to meet with a well-known advertising consultant. The challenge I was facing was how to create more sales during the slow winter months and how to reach customers who were not local. It was suggested that I place an ad for a fabric club in a national quilting magazine, *Quilter's Newsletter*. From that inspiration, I developed the idea for Fabric Finders, a subscription program where I would send fabric swatches, quilting tips, news about new products, and a quilt block pattern each month. My business plan revealed that I would need 300 members to make enough money for my house payment. My next-door neighbor loaned me the money for the start-up, and the ad went into the magazine. In less than two weeks, I had the 300-plus members that I needed to break even, and by the end of the first month I also had the funds to pay back my neighbor. This was the beginning of what would later be called our online presence, and it led to other opportunities.

Early Fabric Finders newsletter and swatches.

Building upon the extensive mailing list developed through Fabric Finders and walk-in customers, I launched a correspondence school where I taught from my book, *Patchwork Quilts Made Easy*, and local instructor, Lawry Thorn, designed and taught a star sampler quilt and monthly Santa Club beginning in 1998. These were some of the first block-of-the-month programs in the country.

In 1999, local contemporary folk art painter John Simpkins, who 30 years later would be the poster artist for the 2006 show, was hired to design the ever-popular quilt *Folk Art Cats*. I continued to place ads in *Quilter's Newsletter* to grow the Stitchin' Post mailing list, a practice that continues to today, but now online.

In 1987, I was hired by Carolie and Tom Hensley, the founders of C&T Publishing, to write a new book, *Fans*. As a young woman, I hated writing term papers, so it's still surprising to me that, all in all, I've written 30 books.

Quilts! Quilts!! Quilts!!!: The Complete Guide to Quiltmaking, by Diana McClun and Laura Nownes (Breckling Press, 1988), was a game changer. It offered a contemporary approach to piecing and quilt design, and I used it as a textbook for my sampler quilt classes. In the end, I made 28 sampler quilts over the time I taught the classes, each one set together differently.

Jennifer Sampou, textile designer and instructor, recalls, "Since my start in fabric design in 1988, I've had the immense privilege of calling Jean and her family my friends. Jean's boundless creative energy and the vibrant community of quilters she has nurtured have truly transformed the quilting industry. Her pioneering spirit and steadfast dedication to the Quilt Show, the store, and education, along with her generosity in sharing her craft, have profoundly inspired my own artistic journey. Jean's commitment has not only shaped the industry but also ignited a shared passion for quilting that continues to unite us, year after year."

LEFT • *Folk Art Cats*, by John Simpkins.

TOP • *Squirrel Crossing* (left) and *Trout Creek* (right), two of many sampler quilts created while teaching my sampler class. *Greetings from Sisters* mural by Katie Daisy and Karen Eland.

At the same time I was cultivating my career and business, the show continued to grow. In 1989, I hired Marina Wood, a local artist and the illustrator on my first book, to create the first official Sisters Outdoor Quilt Show poster. I knew her whimsical style would represent the quilting community well.

The first official poster, 1989, by Marina Wood.

Quilting had entered my life at just the right time. Looking back, it's clear that at the same time, new innovations and a rekindling of interest were breathing life into what had been a vanishing pastime. The quilting industry, our show, and I were in lockstep, marching toward a much larger future. That little show that started with a dozen quilts, casually hung outside my shop, was now hundreds of quilts hung throughout the whole town, with an education program, a formal entry process, and even a show poster. We were picking up steam.

Antique Courthouse Steps quilt. The Sisters Outdoor Quilt Show truly has a come-one-come-all attitude and antique quilts are welcomed alongside those completed months ago.

Visitors stroll through town admiring quilts and visiting local businesses.

The Locals

By 1989, there were approximately 500 quilts hung all throughout town, and people flocked to Sisters from across the state, as well as the West Coast to view them. As word of mouth spread, the show was growing. It was soon to grow even more rapidly. In just fifteen years, Sisters had grown to more than 1,000 folks in the city limits and subdivisions were being built in the forests just outside Sisters. The popularity of the show was rubbing off on the quilt shops located on the main driving routes to Sisters. The quilt shops along the way were purchasing goods, especially for those folks driving to Sisters.

Joyce Coats from Bend, a nearby town, was a big supporter of the Quilt Show. Her husband Bob owned a paving company, and the two of them showed up in Sisters with a truckload of cones for us to use where we needed to close a street or did not want cars parking. We still use those cones today. Joyce also paid for a large advertisement for the show in *Quilter's Newsletter* for several years. Her support is much appreciated.

Dennis McGregor recalls, "I moved to Sisters in 1989 and rented studio space above the Stitchin' Post's original location. I had heard about a big quilt show in the little town and was intrigued. When I met the organizer, Jean Wells, I suggested that she hire me to create a full-color poster to promote the event. She gulped and said okay. The rest, as they say, is history. The poster was well received and followed by many more. I knew nothing about quilts, but I loved the potential for creative ideas that they inspired.

"The town of Sisters's western theme went hand in hand with traditional quilts, leading to several of my poster ideas."

Though Dennis was unaware that we'd had one very early poster, as you can see from his first three posters, Dennis is not only a fabulous painter, but has a great sense of what the Quilt Show is about, from the quilts whirling into town, then dancing on stage (mind you, showing off), to his most famous image, the quilted wagon train. Once spring rolled around

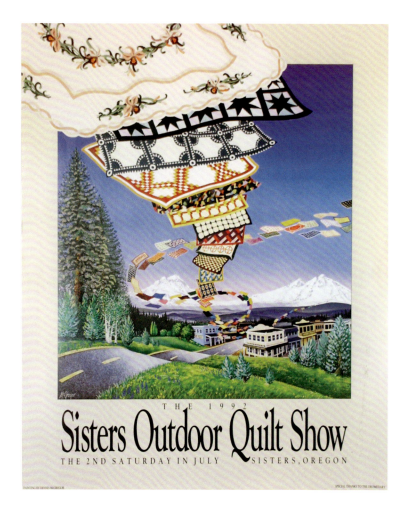

each year, we eagerly awaited Dennis's arrival with a new image. He never disappointed us.

The town continued to grow alongside the show. As new people moved to town, bringing their businesses with them, they found welcoming arms. "When I moved to Sisters in the 1990s from Northern California, I was told I should find a hobby before winter set in," remembers Zoe Willitts, local business owner. "I walked into the Stitchin' Post and immediately felt it was more than just a fabric store. There was a welcoming environment, and I was surrounded by friendship,

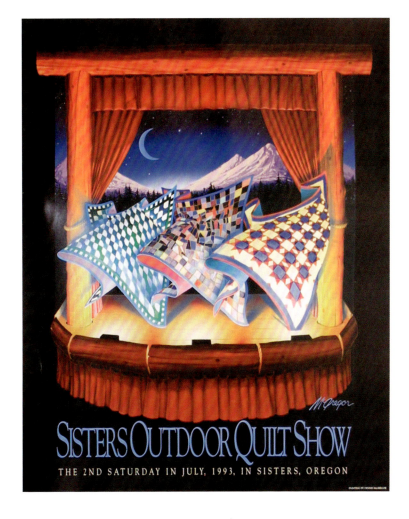
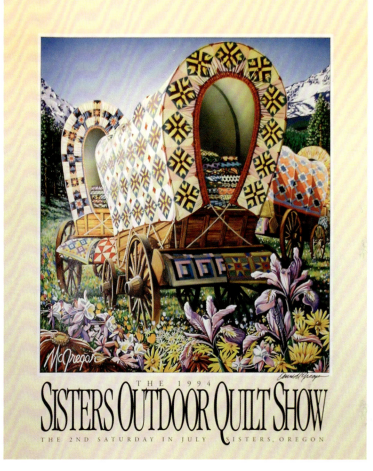

creativity, passion, and enlightenment. The creative juices were awakened in me.

"As I started my massage business, Jean and Valori offered to help in so many ways. They made a beautiful quilt that proudly still hangs in the reception room of Shibui Spa. They gave advice for interior wall hangings and created beautiful shower curtains for the locker rooms. They are true ambassadors for Sisters. They have raised the standings of this community along with a few incredibly talented business owners. We owe so much to these two women and their families."

LEFT • Official 1992 poster, *Whirlwind*, by Dennis McGregor.

MIDDLE • Official 1993 poster, *Quilt Show*, by Dennis McGregor.

RIGHT • Official 1994 poster, *Oregon Trail*, by Dennis McGregor. Prints of this painting are still available for sale on Dennis's website.

Flourishing

In 1994, I wrote *Patchwork Quilts Made Easy*, a comprehensive, hardcover patchwork and quilting book full of a variety of techniques. It became the go-to handbook of basic quilting. The beautiful photographs captured the essence of quilting in Sisters. This book turned out to be one of the first craft books that featured lifestyle photography rather than strictly utilitarian images.

"Jean Wells flows through my creative life in so many ways. I am grateful for the years of inspiration! As I sat down to write a few words to honor the 50th anniversary, I discovered she was the author of one of the very first quilting books I owned, Patchwork Quilts Made Easy. ... *Then I must have seen her on* Simply Quilts *and on the pages of* Quilters Newsletter *magazine as I found my way to art quilting. Teaching at Quilters Affair, visiting the Stitchin' Post and enjoying the magic of the Sisters Outdoor Quilt Show felt like an amazing culmination of both my professional and artistic lives. Her leadership, guidance, support, and gentle spirit were touchstones for me to focus on as my career grew. More than anything, I admire her consistent studio practice and her singular creative vision!"*—Deborah Boschert, instructor and author

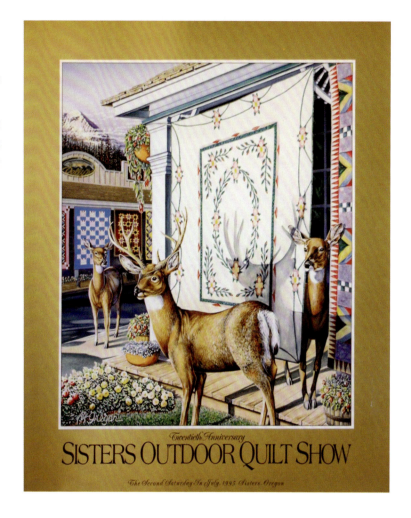

In 1995, the Stitchin' Post was one of the first quilt shops in America to be featured in *Quilt Sampler* magazine. This new publication, written by the editors of *American Patchwork and Quilting* magazine, spotlighted top quilt shops across the country. The magazine sent a writer, a photographer, and an art director to the store in January to create the article. The next summer they sent another group to do a story on the Sisters Outdoor Quilt Show. In that same year, Alex Anderson, author, instructor, and television host, arrived with her crew from the newly minted television show, *Simply Quilts*. During the visit, Alex and her crew took photos and video of quilts with the iconic mountains as a backdrop. Some of these shots became the opening and closing credits for her television show. Before branding was a generally understood concept, the town of Sisters and the Quilt Show were establishing a branded presence. In turn, the added publicity from the magazine and television show brought even more people to the annual show.

LEFT • Official 1995 poster, *Locals*, by Dennis McGregor. Sisters, being next to a national forest, does have town deer that stroll around in the early mornings and evenings.

RIGHT • Official 1996 poster, *Sunflowers*, by Dennis McGregor.

"I am so happy to congratulate you on your 50th anniversary of the Sisters Outdoor Quilt Show and the Stitchin' Post. Our quilt sagas have been so intertwined since Simply Quilts *HGTV launched in 1995.*

"I remember the first time we visited the Sisters show. We were getting footage for our show prior to its launch, and all those quilts outdoors—with the beautiful colors and the gorgeous mountains in the background—were so iconic and perfect that they became part of the opening and closing credits for our TV program. You have said that this recognition helped you to brand Sisters and your annual show, but I was a newbie back then, and you took me under your wing and taught me so much about grace and trust. It was remarkable synergy.

"Since then, we have visited many times, and you have reciprocated as a guest on TheQuiltShow.com. I am grateful for our long and warm friendship, and for all the 'fabricated' adventure."—Alex Anderson, TV personality, instructor, author

One summer, while my daughter Valori was in college, we collaborated on our first book together, *Everything Flowers* (C&T Publishing). At first, because she was a photography major, I hired Val to do all of the photography. However, she was soon interested in the style of quilts that I was making and began designing quilts on the design wall for me to sew up, including the cover quilt and some others for the book. This was the beginning of a series of garden-style books we created together, eventually expanding to include *Through the Garden Gate*, *Along the Garden Path*, and *Garden Inspired Quilts*. Valori's photography not only documented the quilts but also became inspiration for the quilt designs.

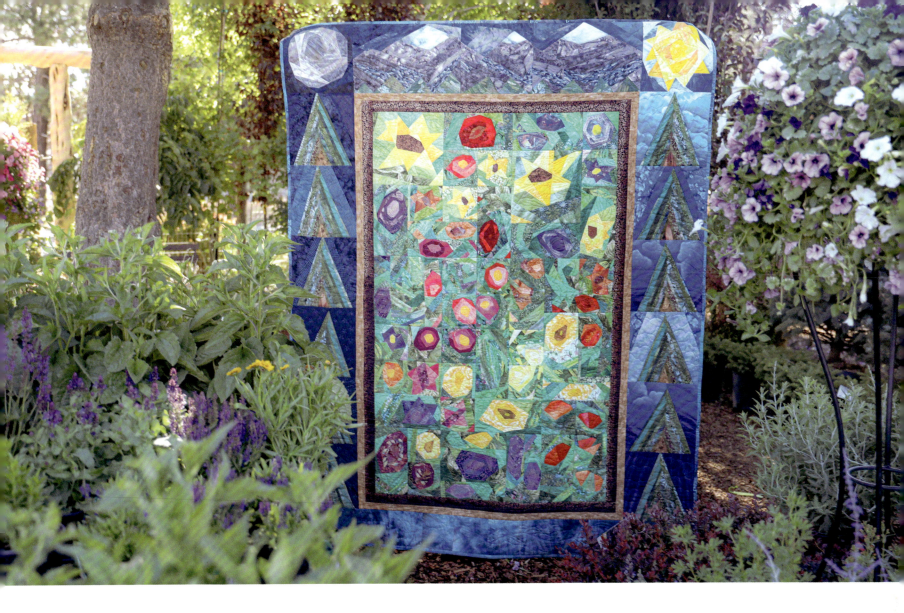

"*It was 1995, the first time I ever heard about the Sisters Outdoor Quilt Show. I had been sewing all my life and quilting since the early '80s, but I didn't know another person who quilted. Imagine the feeling of wonder and amazement walking around the show that year, dodging cars, and just knowing that 'these are my people!' It took four more years to purchase a longarm, then five more years to write my first book and begin teaching at the Quilter's Affair. And then I met Jean Wells. If you want to meet the most generous, sharing, caring, wealth-of-information quilter in the industry, it is Jean. The more [I see] how she innovates and experiments with fabric and thread, it inspires me to follow through with my own ideas, and combine the 'dreaming' and 'doing' stages of design. Thank you so much, Jean, for sharing your time and space, and for making quilting, along with other related arts so available to everyone.*"—Sheila Sinclair Snyder, instructor, author.

LEFT • Valori and I, taken when we were collaborating on garden theme quilt books from 1998 to 2000.

RIGHT • *Memories of My Mother's Garden*, one of Val's first quilts.

Finding Fertile Ground

A New Home

As classically Sisters as the Old Sisters Hotel building was, by the mid-1990s it was clear that we had outgrown the space. In 1997, my now/new husband, John, and I had finished building Pine Tree Square, a new commercial building for the Stitchin' Post and two other tenants, just down Cascade Avenue from the original location. Also, in 1997, I was inducted into the Crafttrends Independent Retailer's Hall of Fame, and only the next year, I was humbled to receive the Michael Kyle Award of Excellence at the International Quilt Festival in Houston, Texas.

LEFT • Official 1997 poster, *Log Cabin Settlers*, by Dennis McGregor.

RIGHT • Quilts across the front of the new Stitchin' Post building, blowing in the breeze.

Around this time, Valori moved back to Oregon from the East Coast after graduation and applied for a job at the Stitchin' Post. The books and notions buyer had given notice, and I hired Valori. One of the first things she suggested was that the store needed a website. That became one of her tasks, as well as bringing the staff up to date on the internet. Under her guidance, the store created a fabulous website, and we were soon connecting with a whole new, larger, more distant, and often younger, group of customers. Across the country, younger women were taking up quilting, and the threads of a modern movement were emerging. Fabric colors became clearer and brighter, and the scale of designs on printed fabrics became larger. It was a magical time!

As Valori settled in at the store it began taking on a fresh new look as she put her artistic talent to work in displays, product selection, store samples, and the website. The Stitchin' Post has always been a trend-setting business in the quilting world.

Official 1998 poster, *McGregor's Garden*, by Dennis McGregor.

LEFT • Quilts by the Quilter's Affair instructors were originally displayed in a tent.

RIGHT • Quilts organized and stacked prior to hanging.

While the Stitchin' Post was launching into the digital scene, the friends, family, and community of Sisters continued to lend a hand to the show. June Jaeger recollects, "In 1998, I formed my own quilt hanging team, which still hangs quilts with me 27 years later. My team of seven to ten women all come from Prineville, a nearby town. I have now added eight to ten [more] people as my section size has grown. We climb ladders, clothespin the quilts to covered wires, fold and refold quilts. The placement team works behind the scenes prior to the show, placing the quilts in categories of style and color. They are processed and pinned with [the quiltmaker's] personal story and a ribbon. Then they go into bags labeled with the location where they will be hung. I pick up my team's bags at 6:30 in the morning as the sun peeks over the pine trees. Bags are laid out on sidewalks, and one quilt at a time is carefully taken from the bag and handed to the team member on the ladder and hung with clothespins. Spectators ooh and ahh as the quilts emerge from the bags and drape the town in color.

"At 4 o'clock in the afternoon, the reverse happens. The teams begin taking quilts down and carefully folding and bagging them. They return to be checked in and alphabetized for pickup the next day. Without all of the dedicated volunteers who love Quilt Show, it could not happen."

Each year, the quilting community in Sisters grows, both by quilters relocating and through the magic of Sisters turning new residents into quilters. Betsy Menefee recalls, "In the winter of 1999, not long after my family moved to Central Oregon, I happened upon a PBS show about quilting and impulsively decided to try my hand at it. I had no idea that one of the most renowned quilt stores in the country was just a few miles down the road and that within a few months I would join the throngs of dedicated quilters taking class after class at the Stitchin' Post and indulging my craving for beautiful fabrics. More important, I would meet the woman who became not only a mentor but one of my dearest friends.

"It didn't take long for me to inquire about working at the Stitchin' Post and eventually suggesting to Jean that she could use a personal assistant—perhaps I might fit the bill? While reminiscing about those years, all I can say is that they were incredibly fun, energizing, and inspirational. During that time, Jean lured those masters of color and quilting, who I refer to as the 'Mick Jaggers' of the quilting world, to teach at the Quilter's Affair. Kaffe Fassett and Brandon Mably, Gwen Marston, Janet Bolton, and the amazing Gees Bend Quilters. Of course, Jean Wells is included in that group.

"To this day, I can't drive through Sisters without stopping at the Stitchin' Post knowing that there will be at least a fat quarter, if not yards of fabric, that must be added to my stash. If I'm really lucky, Jean will be there ready to be whisked off so that we can catch up over a cup of tea or lunch. Cheers and congratulations to Jean, Val, and the Stitchin' Post! But especially, thank you for spreading joy and enthusiasm to the throngs of quilters and knitters who've been lucky enough to venture into your world."

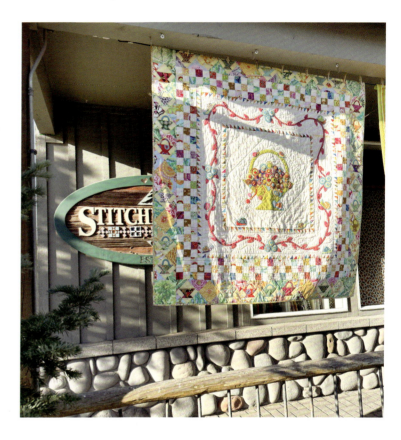

At a Snail's Pace medallion quilt, by Betsy Menefee.

"Jean has always stood out to me as the courageous creator of an event that inspired and galvanised the world of quilting. Recognising that the creative tribes of craftspeople would respond to an event glorifying their output and having the tenacity to make [it] happen are to be saluted. I am delighted to be included several times in this wonderful happening in the beautiful Oregon High Desert.

"One of the most amazing things that happened to me while directing a workshop in the Stitchin' Post is seared in my memory. As I was halfway through my class of patchwork, a shipment of fabric arrived at the store, including a new print of mine featuring Paperweight called Millefiore. I told the class that one of the bolts was my favourite colouring of this pattern, and in fifteen minutes the entire bolt was purchased by the enthusiastic crowd. I've never had that happen before or since! This illustrated to me what a powerful creative atmosphere Jean and her daughter, Valori, have given birth to, drawing so many people to this small country town and giving them space and encouragement to realise their talents."—Kaffe Fassett, instructor, artist, and fabric designer for FreeSpirit Fabrics

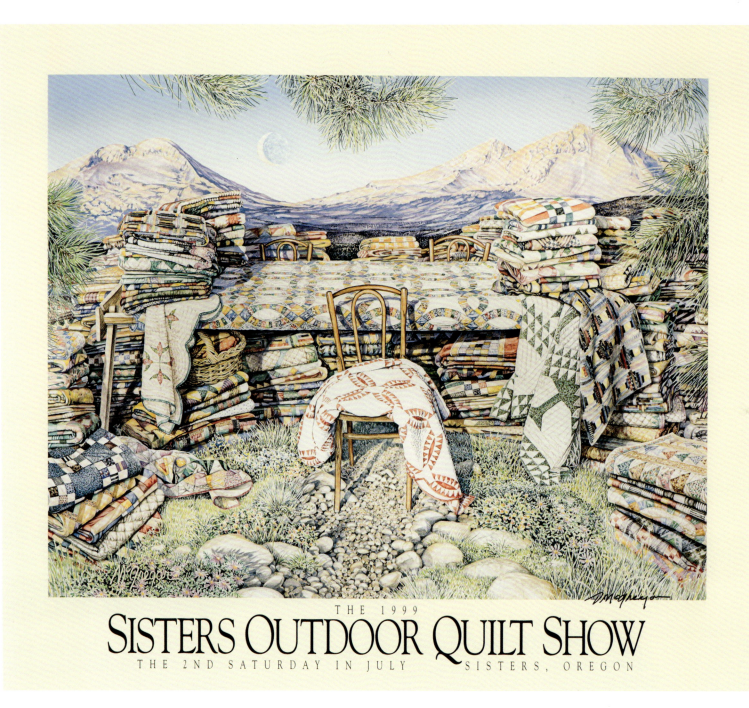

In 1999, the Chamber of Commerce named the Stitchin' Post Business of the Year. It was an immense honor. The staff and my entire family surprised me and attended the event—I'd had no idea what was up!

Official 1999 poster, *Cascade of Quilts*, by Dennis McGregor. I collected all of these quilts for Dennis to use for the poster image, but he did not let me see it until it was finished. I was so thrilled seeing my family quilts and a collection of antique ones in this poster image.

LEFT • I am reviewing the current version of The Book. It contains a photograph of every location in Sisters where quilts can be hung, complete with vertical and horizontal measurements of each space.

RIGHT • Granddaughter Olivia and I sorting quilts.

The 25th Anniversary

With the year 2000 show coming up, I decided it was time to create what we coined The Book, which was a comprehensive guide to where to hang each quilt for the show. In hindsight, it was an ambitious project, though in some ways, so was the show itself. As recalled by retired employee Joyce Boyd, "One morning at the Stitchin' Post, Jean grabbed Barbara Ferguson and myself to walk around town from place to place where the wires were hung on buildings to pin the quilts to. She had this vision that if we could photograph each of these locations and include measurements, it would organize the quilt hanging. I was overwhelmed, but I slowly made it happen. And remember, that was done before digital cameras. I was always going to Photos in a Flash, picking up new prints, and hand-gluing them in the first The Book. Twenty-five years later, the book is still in place with digital updates."

Finding Fertile Ground

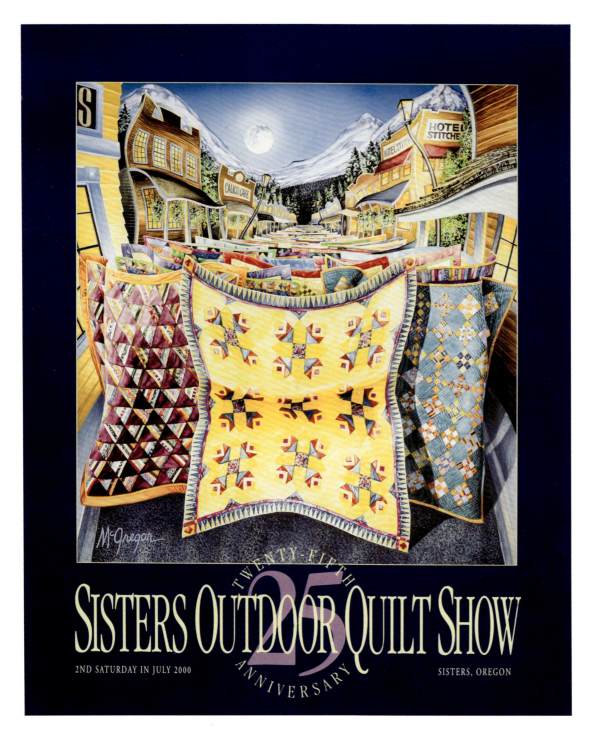

Official 2000 poster, *Parade*, by Dennis McGregor. What better way to celebrate an anniversary than a quilted parade!

"When the 25th anniversary of the show approached, Jean asked me to come up with some ideas of ways to celebrate it. I knew that there were hundreds of quilters hanging around town with nothing to do (so I thought), and maybe they could be part of it," notes Dennis McGregor. "I designed a 'human quilt' which would use quilters as participants—891 of them. Turns out they were all very busy with classes and such, so it had to happen at 6:00 a.m., the day of the show."

Dennis designed the human quilt, picked the colors, and engineered the 36″ × 36″ blocks by stapling wood slats to each end of a piece of fabric. FreeSpirit Fabrics donated the fabric yardage to make the blocks. The East of the Cascades Quilters Guild in Sisters held a work party to create them and roll each one up and put it in order in a tall box. A local videographer, who'd been a pioneer in photographing extreme sports, agreed to film the event.

On July 7, 2000, at 6:00 a.m., 891 people came together in the early morning hours to kick off the celebration of the 25th anniversary of the Sisters Outdoor Quilt Show. Even my husband's golfing buddies came to help out! The high school football field was gridded, and Dennis was on the microphone. We all stood at attention, and when he told us to hold up our blocks, we all did. It was so magical!

Dennis reminisces, "It was an epic challenge to create and orchestrate, and [it] required an army of volunteers. It was a big success, the likes of which [would] never be repeated. It was a lot of work!"

The Human Quilt.

Finding Fertile Ground

becoming Today's Show

As the Show grew in size, so did the complexity of quilt displays. Each year the Sisters—
Camp Sherman Fire Department helps hang quilts on the side of the Stitchin' Post.

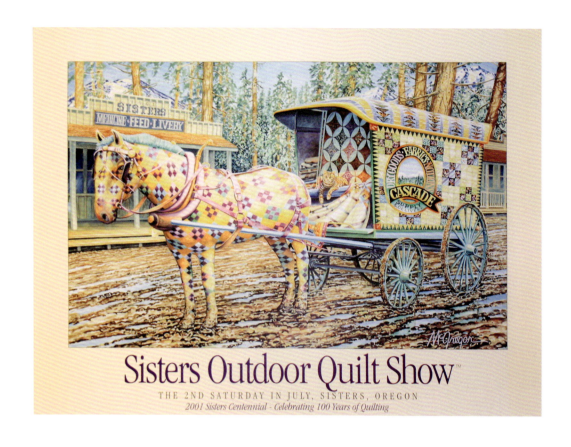

Official 2001 poster, *Nine Patch Horse*, by Dennis McGregor.

The Tipping Point

Now at 700 quilts and thousands of attendees, we were approaching a tipping point, though we didn't quite realize it at the time. Valori's and my careers, the success of the shop, and the popularity of the show were all building apace, and it would soon become apparent that something had to give.

In the late 1990s, a new generation of quilters began to look for more ways to add their own creativity to their quilts, giving rise to the art of free-motion quilting, which truly took off in popularity in the early 2000s. Books started being published and workshops taught on the subject. It is still popular today. Valori was fearless when it came to free-motion quilting. She said it was like sketching in her sketchbook.

Also in the early years of this century, paper piecing became very popular as quilters looked for additional ways to add complexity and versatility to their quilting. Val and I began experimenting with paper pieced New York Beauty–style quilts inspired by Karen K. Stone's famous quilt, taught in her 1995 self-published book *New York Beauty*.

In just seven short years, Valori wrote three books: *Stitch 'n Flip Quilts* in 2000, *Radiant New York Beauties* in 2003, and *Simple Start-Stunning Finish* in 2007. Around this same time, the Stitchin' Post began hosting retreats at Lake Creek Lodge, a local resort located in Camp Sherman,

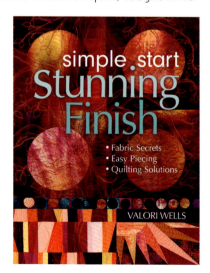

 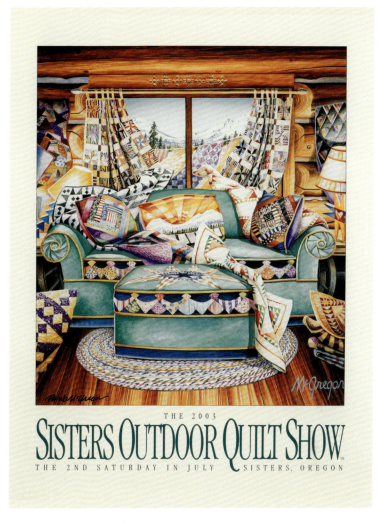

LEFT • Official 2002 poster, *Patriot's Needle*, by Dennis McGregor.

RIGHT • Official 2003 poster, *Lodge*, by Dennis McGregor.

---

twelve miles down the road from Sisters. Nationally known teachers were invited to give workshops at this beautiful spot nestled among the ponderosa pine trees.

By 2003, I found myself overwhelmed with the management of the store, running the Quilter's Affair education program, and producing the Sisters Outdoor Quilt Show.

I met with my accountant, who suggested I turn the Quilt Show into a nonprofit and hire an executive director. After much research, I did just that and hired Ann Richardson for the position. Together, we put the wheels in motion, chose a board of directors, and put together a plan for the event that is still in place today.

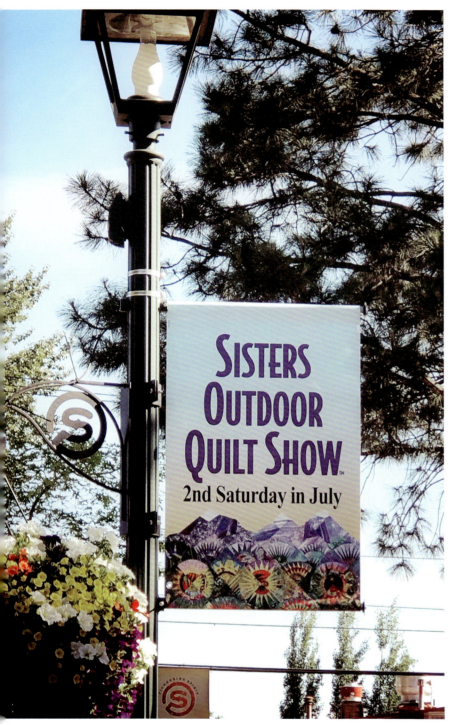

Ann Richardson remembers the early days fondly. "With a business and financial background but zero nonprofit experience, I closed my eyes, held my breath and jumped into the role of executive director for Sisters Outdoor Quilt Show in 2003," Richardson says. "Jean and I established the Quilt Show as a nonprofit organization—formally named SSJ, Inc. (for second Saturday of July)—to educate and inspire the public about the art of quilting and to enhance the economic vitality of our community. I knew nothing about running a nonprofit, but I quickly learned, and the eleven years I spent leading SOQS were some of the happiest and most rewarding of my working career. It wasn't until I took on that job that I truly understood the meaning of community. Just try putting on an event that brings over 10,000 tourists to your small town, all in one day, and do it without the entire community's enthusiastic support. Without the quilters willing to trust us with their treasures; without the hundreds of volunteer hours to prepare, hang, watch over, and return those quilts; without the generosity of local businesses to financially support the show and allow us to hang quilts on their buildings; and without the myriad entities that manage trash, traffic, and safety, there would be no Quilt Show. Sisters may be a small community, but when we come together, we accomplish really big things."

LEFT • Second Saturday in July is a phrase seen frequently throughout town.

RIGHT • In the early years of the show Cascade Avenue was closed to allow visitors to throng our little downtown.

Over the 50 years of the quilt show, it has only rained once, and only for fifteen minutes. Everyone grabbed quilts and dashed into businesses. It was spontaneous, and in the end, there was no damage to any of the quilts. Talk about unity!

The advent of managing the show as a nonprofit freed up time and creative energy to add new vitality to the show, and in the years following 2003, many new and exciting programs would become part of the annual tradition. Jan McGowan, former member of the board of directors says it best: "At first, the event grew organically, nurtured by its founder and a few passionate friends and family members. Over the years, the show has developed into a strong nonprofit organization, demonstrating a level of planning and sophistication often missing in small rural communities. Its impact today is felt by businesses throughout Central Oregon, including the hotels, restaurants, and shops frequented by show attendees, and by its partner organizations and beneficiaries, especially the schools, in Sisters. SOQS has truly become a model for successful community arts organizations, recognized and admired both near and far."

As in many nonprofit organizations, executive directors come and go. We have been very fortunate to have hired the right person for the job at hand. As the organization has grown, its needs have changed. Dawn M. Boyd, the current director, has been able to expand the fundraising that is essential to nonprofits. She is a talented grant writer, as well as a wonderful ambassador to the community organizations and in forging relationships with the city, sheriff, and fire departments, and Oregon Department of Transportation.

Boyd shares that "The Quilt Show [today] continues multiple avenues to raise its funds for the Quilt Show operations, including long-standing traditions: business sponsorships, foundation and government grants, quilter registration fees, the WISH Upon a Card program, a weekly fundraiser during Quilter's Affair week, a yearly Raffle Quilt, a Holiday fundraiser, and donations from our Friends of the Show."

Every year the Stitchin' Post issues an employee challenge and our employees rise to the occassion. Visitors can see all the amazing employee quilts on the side of the Stitchin' Post.

Fresh Features

In 2004, longarm quilting machines were introduced by several vendors. They soon were preferred by makers to hand quilting, but the majority of quilters did not have a space for them or couldn't afford them. That year, a number of quilts entered in the show all had a clamshell pattern quilting motif, but since then, operators have found ways to personalize quilting designs to each quilt top and have created some stunning quilts. We now showcase both machine and hand-quilted quilts each summer.

Sisters, Oregon—Five Decades of Quilting in America

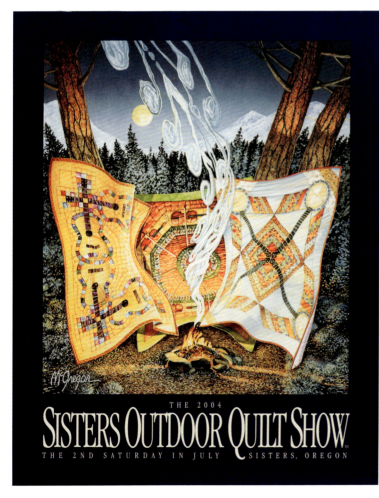

TOP • Cousins Braden and Olivia strolling up Cascade Avenue on Quilt Show day.

LEFT • Official 2004 poster, *Campfire Quilts*, by Dennis McGregor.

BOTTOM • Official 2005 poster, *Hands All Around the World Coming Together in Quilting*, by Dennis McGregor.

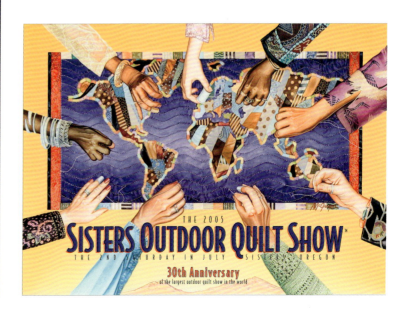

Planning the Show Day quilt displays is a monumental task requiring a lot of space and numerous man hours.

The Planning

During the planning for the 2005 show, my son, Jason Wells, suggested the use of barcodes to identify each quilt. From then on, each quilt has received a barcode when it is checked in. The barcode appears on the information sheet pinned to the quilt and on the label attached to the back of the quilt. The code is scanned into a database, allowing us to print a directory so entrants can look up where their quilt is hung. Once a place has been selected for the quilt to be displayed, that same barcode is placed on the relevant page in The Book. That barcode follows the quilt through the entire process. At the end of the show, once the quilt has been taken down and returned to the office, the barcode is scanned again and the quilt is then sorted alphabetically for pickup. This is valuable as it ensures that we always know where the quilt is.

LEFT • *The Book provides the logistical planning.*

RIGHT • *Each page helps volunteers visualize the available space, understand the dimensions, and select just the right quilts to hang in each spot.*

Sisters, Oregon—Five Decades of Quilting in America

Volunteers are what fuels the Show. From left to right, Deb Meier, me, Donna Rice, Betsy Sparks, Ginn Staines, Leah Pahlmeyer, Janet Roshak, Liz Weeks, Carol Dixon, Marion Shimoda, Kathy Jasper, and Janet M. Tetzlaff.

As a small nonprofit, the Sisters Outdoor Quilt Show runs out of a small office space during the majority of the year. But when it comes time to begin collecting quilts, the headquarters are relocated into a larger space in Sisters. Over the years, a number of businesses have allowed SOQS to take over their warehouse space for five weeks, from the middle of June through the week following the show.

Calling on volunteers and high school students, the transition from one office space to another includes setting up large rows of tables to organize the quilts. Each quilt arrives and is checked in, receiving its quilt registration tag and barcode, and it's then folded to specified size by a willing volunteer. The quilts are next semi-organized by size, color, and style. Each step in the process has been fine-tuned over the past 50 years, and each quilt is taken care of with much love and admiration.

Once all of the quilts have arrived for the show and have been processed for hanging, the fun begins for the placement team of ten people! A page from The Book is pulled and given to a team member, and they look for quilts that are the correct size for the available space and that have something in common with their neighbors. They create a grouping that has something in common, such as a theme, a dominant color, or a definite pattern. The grouped quilts are then stacked and checked in, barcodes are added to The Book, and the group of quilts is bagged and the bag labeled with the same information that appears on the page from The Book. It runs like clockwork.

LEFT · *Each grouping of quilts has something in common, from color to composition, complicating the planning.*

RIGHT · *Once selections are final, quilts are bagged up to protect them on their way to their hanging destination.*

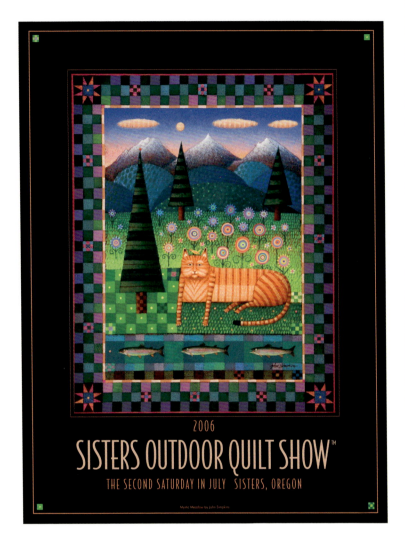
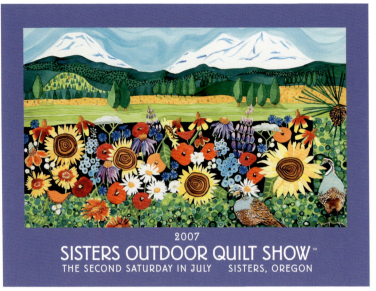
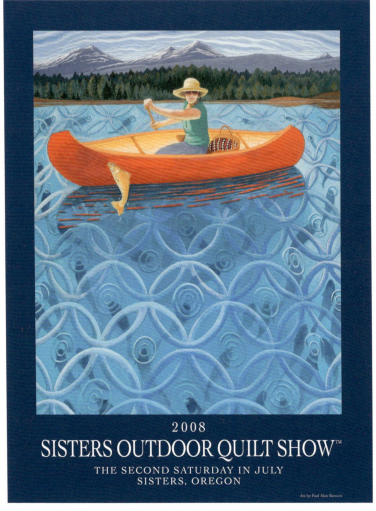

LEFT • Official 2006 poster, *Mystic Meadow*, by John Simpkins.

TOP RIGHT • Official 2007 poster, *Nature's Inspiration*, by Kathy Deggendorfer.

BOTTOM RIGHT • Official 2008 poster, *Wedding Ring Blues*, by Paul Alan Bennett.

Quilting as an art form continued to build and grow through the first decade and more of the 21st century. Reflecting that popularity and how the show had grown symbiotically with the town and community, in 2007 I was awarded Citizen of the Year by the Sisters Chamber of Commerce for my work and devotion to the Sisters Outdoor Quilt Show.

In 2009, I wrote *Intuitive Color and Design*, stepping into the improv quilting world. I also offered my first five-day workshop on these techniques at the Stitchin' Post. I still offer this workshop, and many more, today.

Linda Weick, Sisters resident and participant in that first workshop, remembers it this way: "There were twelve of us in that first Intuitive Color and Design workshop. We came from Washington, D.C.; North Carolina; Idaho; Arizona; California; and Oregon to learn from Jean Wells …, the master of color, design, ruler-less cutting, and piecing. I signed up for the five-day class to immerse myself in learning new techniques and stretching my use of color, but [I] really had no idea what was going to happen. From the moment we introduced ourselves, and for the remainder of the week, we worked hard, laughed, explored, and bonded as a group.

"Jean was more than just a teacher; she was a generous participant, pushing us to explore all of the techniques that she had developed. We began the exercise by choosing fabrics from solid-colored strips that Jean had supplied for us. I was conservative in my choices and chose mostly neutrals. Then we had to come back and pick a bit of poison. By the time I reached the table, not much was left, and I ended up with bubble gum pink. Yikes. I incorporated small slices of this fabric into my project and WOW! The whole thing came to life.

"Fourteen years later, I still love that piece and it is on the wall in my sewing room where I have a daily opportunity to remember that great experience. The 2010 group continued to meet the next five years for workshops with Jean. Six members of that original group now live in Sisters where we continue to be in awe of Jean's artistry, generosity, and energy."

Left to right, Mary Stieweg, Martha Pfair Sanders, and Betty Gientke's quilts are part of the 2024 Journeys special exhibit. The Journeys are a group of ten quilters who have been meeting for many years.

Around this same time, a group of women who wanted to work more intuitively approached me. We formed a group and named ourselves Journeys, as we all felt we were on a magical journey in quilting. The group still exists today. Our meetings focus on "art talk," and we hold an exhibit of our work at the show each year.

"What a gift you have given to quilters with your 50 years of commitment to education and sharing of your vision, talent, and expertise. You should be very proud of the inspiring body of work that you have produced in your own journey and the way your encouragement and influence have helped shape the creative lives of quilters and artists from Sisters, Central Oregon, and well beyond. You can talk to quilters worldwide, and they will all know of the Sisters Outdoor Quilt Show. I'm so fortunate it's in my own backyard! With gratitude and love from your friend and student."—Val Shewell, volunteer and student

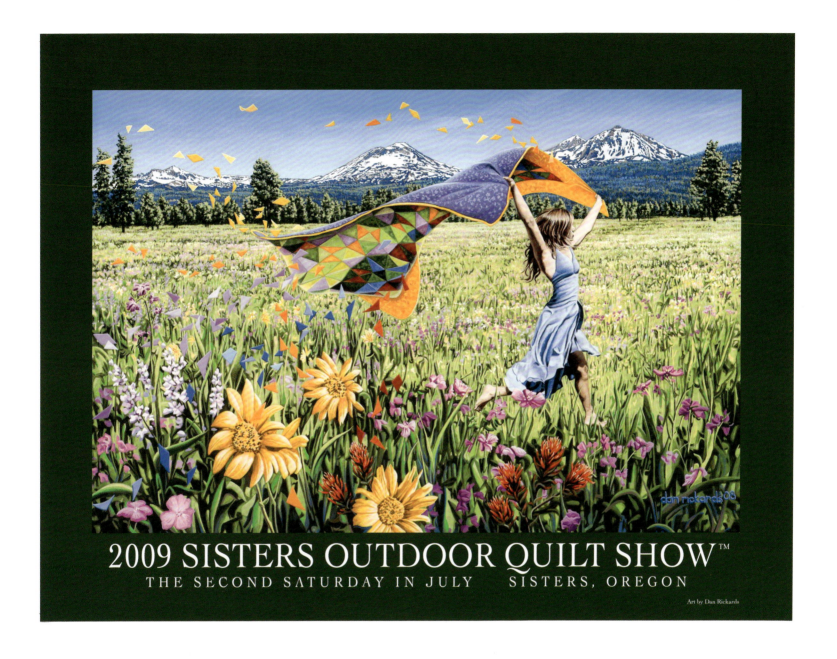

Official 2009 poster, *Summer Bliss*, by Dan Rickards.

Dan Rickards and his wife, Julia, have created the Rickards Art Gallery and Open Door restaurant in Sisters. They are both strong supporters of the show and host a textile artist each year during the show. Their restaurant and gallery is located on a lovely piece of property that they have developed, featuring outside seating and three small cottages for dining. Dan is also responsible for creating The Storybook Project (page 78).

In 2009, the board of directors voted to launch a series of yearly special exhibits to showcase the talents of our Central Oregon quilters and some of the visiting instructors who teach at the Quilter's Affair. Throughout the show, visitors are treated to a more in-depth look at the work of a variety of quilters honored as the featured quilter, featured machine quilter, inspirational instructor, FivePine indoor showcase artist, and gallery artist. The featured quilters special exhibit continues yearly.

Carol Dixon, SOQS board member, shares her perspective on this honor: "Before I knew the difference between a log cabin and a flying geese quilt block, I would drive annually to the Saturday Sisters Outdoor Quilt Show simply to appreciate the color, design, and beauty of the pieces of fabric art flowing outdoors in the summer breeze in charming downtown Sisters. My quilting journey has been largely personal and private. After moving to Sisters in 1992, I took my first quilting class from Lawry Thorn at the Stitchin' Post. I was immediately hooked! My husband and I travel extensively, and I discovered quilting as a means to create a visible chronicle of our foreign adventures. I made many quilts and found the creative process of choosing a design, selecting fabric, and putting together a travel theme especially compelling and satisfying. The only time these quilts were exposed to the public was when I would take the trip to the Stitchin' Post to choose the perfect border, binding, or backing fabric to complete it. During more than one of these visits, Jean Wells happened to see my work. Imagine my surprise when Jean contacted me and asked if I would be the featured quilter for the 2021 show! Jean Wells! Me! I insisted she visit my home to see more of my work to judge if I was, indeed, 'good enough' for such recognition.

"My son, Slater, is in the film industry and added to my honor by creating a professional-level video of me and highlighting my quilting journey. He created a personalized business card with a QR code to memorialize the event. The 2021 show experience is one I will never forget."

Dancing Fans, by Judith Beaver. In 2024, Judith Beaver was the featured machine quilter.

"Being the featured machine quilter in 2023 for the Sisters Outdoor Quilt Show was the best experience for me. I had the opportunity to speak with all of the guests about how I study the quilts and try to plan a design that will complete the story they are portraying in their work. It is the last layer of design in each of the quilts I work on. It was just an amazing day for me," remembers Annette Caldwell, purchasing manager for the Stitchin' Post.

Local quilter Kris Lang shares that "The Sisters Outdoor Quilt show has a special place in my heart as a longtime Central Oregonian. In 2023, I had the privilege to be the featured quilt artist at the Rickards Gallery during the week of Quilt Show activities, and I have participated throughout the years in the Studio Art Quilt Associates exhibit, Undercover Quilters, and Mt. Bachelor Guild exhibits at the show. The professionalism and care are so evident in the Quilter's Affair and Quilt Show, and you feel a sense of family when you participate."

Due in part to my work with my community through the annual Quilt Show, in 2010 I was inducted into the Quilting Hall

TOP • *The Wedding Quilt*, by Jean Wells. This quilt inspired the design of the poster.

BOTTOM • Official 2010 poster, quilts by Jean Wells. To celebrate the 35th anniversary of the Quilt Show, several of my quilts were featured on the show poster, showcasing my journey in quiltmaking and design.

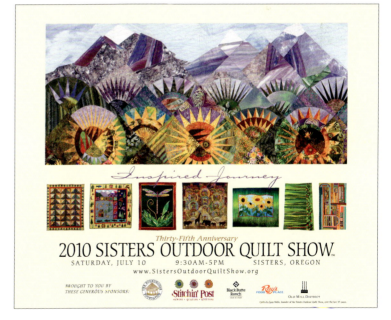

LEFT • The high desert sun illuminates *Fun with Strips*, by Christa Rinne.

RIGHT • *Coxcomb and Currents* was created by Joanne Myers and hung in the iconic Village Green Park in Sisters where the teachers' quilt exhibit is showcased each year.

of Fame in Marion, Indiana. My husband, John; my sister, June Jaeger; my children, Jason and Valori; and my grandchildren, Braden and Olivia traveled with me to the event. Little did I know that a Chicago group of quilters who attended the Quilt Show that year would come to help celebrate the occasion with me and my family.

Barbara Myers Fortman remembers the 2010 Quilt Show because of how important it was for her mother, Joanne. "Joanne Myers and her husband Horace moved to Bend, Oregon, in 1986. Being from the flatlands of the Midwest, Joanne couldn't put her ideas onto fabric fast enough. She was instantly amazed by the Cascade Mountains and began making landscape quilts. She met Jean at the Stitchin' Post,

and they became fast friends. Joanne volunteered at the Quilt Show, taught workshops at Quilter's Affair, and was a featured quilter one year. She also became very active in the Mt. Bachelor Quilt Guild and always opened her home to anyone who wanted to learn to quilt. She was a prolific quilter and dear friend of the show.

"She also delved into the history of the quilt and often volunteered at the High Desert Quilt Museum. She arrived in Bend in '86 with an inherited family quilt top *Coxcomb and Currents*. She loved handwork and hand-quilted the well-preserved top, finishing it in 2010. It hung in her special exhibit as Inspirational Instructor that year."

Sisters, Oregon—Five Decades of Quilting in America

New Horizons

While some things were about to change, and the show would begin growing by leaps and bounds, some things remained the same. Donna Rice shares that "Bright and early in the morning of Quilt Show, eighteen teams (150 volunteers) gather and ascend on the streets of Sisters. Armed with ladders, rags to clean wires if necessary, clothespins, signage, and more important, large labeled plastic bags filled with the quilts to be hung, the process takes approximately two hours to hang 1,000 quilts. By 9:00 a.m., the city of Sisters is transformed into a magical village." My daughter, Valori, likens it to "magical butterflies emerging from sleep."

Hanging team at work on Quilt Show day.

In 2008, Betsy Menefee helped me contact the Gee's Bend Quilters of Alabama to see if they would like to be our guests at the show. Little did we know that they would come and teach some workshops, too. In 2011, the Gee's Bend Quilters made their first of three trips to Sisters for the Sisters Outdoor Quilt Show. What fun we all had listening to the beautiful voices of the women singing as they stitched and learning from them as they taught their hand-piecing classes and shared their natural creativity. They shared a video with us and talked about their lives and about how much stitching and quilting held them together during hard times. They told us it was the first time they had attended a quilt show and taught classes as well. They thoroughly enjoyed their time in our little town.

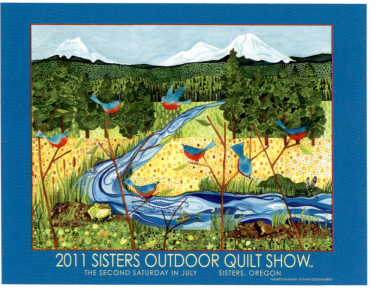

LEFT TOP • My five grandchildren began attending the quilt show at an early age. The extended family has placed cones early in the morning, repaired frames, hung and taken down quilts, and acted as ambassadors. My grandchildren have also worked at Quilter's Affair and the Stitchin' Post.

LEFT BOTTOM • Official 2011 poster, *Nature's Symphony*, by Kathy Deggendorfer.

RIGHT • Official 2012 poster, *Go to Town*, by Kathy Deggendorfer.

The Men Behind the Quilts *Calendars*

Three times—in 2012, 2014, and 2016—Sisters Outdoor Quilt Show initiated a project to create an eighteen-month *Men Behind the Quilts* calendar. Eighteen men from the community donated their likenesses to help raise money for the Quilt Show. Eighteen quilters from the community and some of the Quilter's Affair teachers donated their time and talent by creating quilts for the calendar. The models were all active in the Sisters community as business owners, teachers, and civic leaders, and they were interviewed for a sidebar in the calendar.

The Quilt Show attendees visited many of the volunteers' businesses, and the models participated in the fundraising auction for the quilts. We love supporting our community with our Quilt Show activities.

The Thursday before the show, we held an event and raffled off the quilts, all to raise additional funds for the show.

The Men Behind the Quilt Calendar *featured not only quilts, but the businesses of the models.*

Sisters, Oregon—Five Decades of Quilting in America

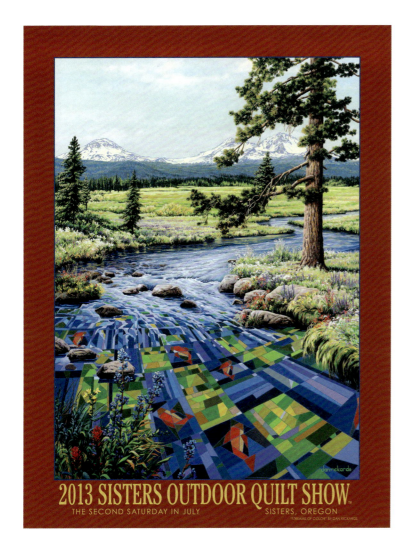

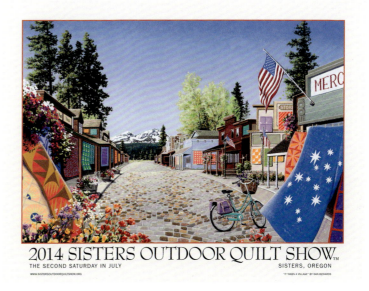

Education and inspiration continues to be the foundation of the Stitchin' Post, Quilter's Affair, and the Sisters Outdoor Quilt Show. In the mid-2000s, my teaching expanded to include giving workshops and lectures across the United States, as well as in England, France, Japan, South Africa, and Taiwan. As I traveled the globe, word spread and images of quilts hanging outdoors in Sisters country became widely seen. Little did I realize that in doing so, I was branding Sisters.

In 2013, our first executive director, Ann Richardson, retired and the board of directors hired Jeanette Pilak to take her place, just in time to begin planning for the 40th anniversary.

LEFT • Official 2013 poster, *Streams of Color*, by Dan Rickards.

TOP RIGHT • Jean and Valori were commissioned to create *Five Pine* for the Willitts family and the FivePine Lodge.

BOTTOM RIGHT • Official 2014 poster, *It Takes a Village*, by Dan Rickards.

"Quilting, military service, and charitable support are all proud American traditions—bringing people together around common causes," wrote Susan Stafford in a 2014 article about the special exhibit Quilted in Honor. Sponsored by Island Batiks, the exhibit featured 50 celebrity quilters with the goal of paying tribute to, and financially benefiting military personnel and their families. We involved our local Veterans of Foreign Wars members and invited them to see the quilts and local veterans held a short ceremony honoring those who had lost their lives in battle. "For the Troops" *Sisters Outdoor Quilt Show* program, 2014.

In 2015, the Sisters Outdoor Quilt Show celebrated its 40th anniversary. That year we would host thousands of attendees to wander the streets and parks and take in 1,000 quilts. Quilter's Affair had grown to twenty workshops per day.

Instructor Lou Shafer likens one of her favorite Quilter's Affair classes to the mythical *Brigadoon*. Similar to how the magical Scottish village comes to life once every 100 years, "Once each year, magic surely takes over, and the little East of the Cascades community is transformed into a mecca for quilters and quilt-lovers from all over the world!

"Saturday mornings start early and the magic *is* in the air as staff, faculty, and tons of volunteers gather for directions to hang quilts all over town. In less than two hours, Sisters is dressed for a day of inspiration, color, crowds, and amazement.

"My sister Jan and I were never sure how we were lucky enough to lead the hanging of the Teachers' Tent exhibit and *then* spend the day meeting, greeting, and demoing hand quilting, but we sure loved every second of it! And, in 2004, we were honored as featured teachers in the Teachers' Tent."

I joined the Studio Art Quilt Associates international organization as a juried member in 2015 and found the group to be very stimulating. When the state of Oregon was looking for a representative, I asked Betty Daggett, a quilting friend from Portland, to co-represent with me. We attended a national convention and came back to Oregon with the idea of forming pods, or mini groups, that could meet on a monthly basis. I put the word out in Central Oregon, and within a year, there were 30 members meeting monthly at the Stitchin' Post. During Betty's and my term, we organized a state convention and regional juried show that traveled the state of Oregon.

In 2017, the second edition of my *Intuitive Color and Design* was published—my 30th book! We also launched the Storybook Project, a physical book featuring quilted pages, which visitors can still find today as a show feature.

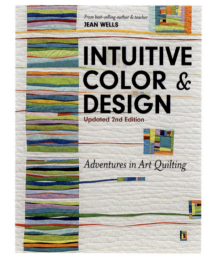

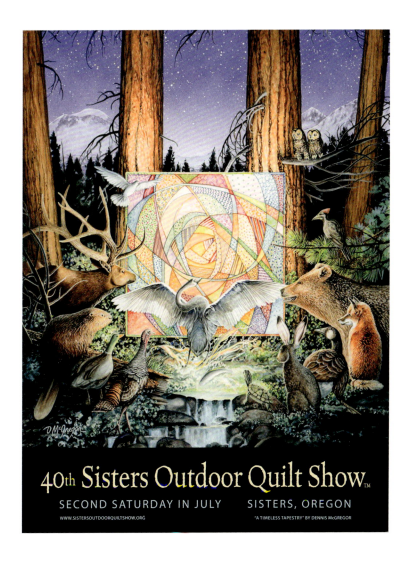
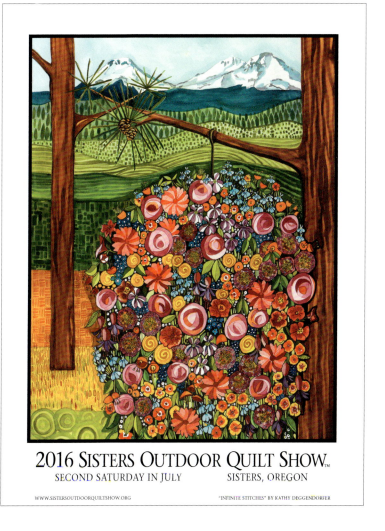

LEFT • Official 2015 poster, *A Timeless Tapestry*, by Dennis McGregor.

RIGHT • Official 2016 poster, *Infinite Stitches*, by Kathy Deggendorfer.

The Storybook Project

Some years see the advent of a new show feature. In 2017, the first of the Storybook Projects took place. "A giant storybook is literally filled with quilts. It was a natural extension of the theme and the inspiration for the 2017 Sisters Outdoor Quilt Show poster by artist Dan Rickards. That same year, art was translated to reality and a 2' × 3' leather tooled book was created by Dan and filled with wall-size quilts created by ten Central Oregon textile artists.

"Pages of the book were turned during the week before Quilt Show and again on Quilt Show day to an admiring audience. Each quilt, donated by the maker, was sold with 100 percent of the proceeds benefiting the nonprofit Sisters Outdoor Quilt Show.

"The following year, the book was filled again with new quilts, each a unique piece of art. The Metolius River, favorite walks, children at play, and Paris gardens are just a few of the subjects illustrated in the quilts.

"Now a beloved Quilt Show tradition, the Storybook Project continues to showcase work by quilt artists who love and support the Quilt Show. The quilts become a beloved keepsake for their purchasers who take home art and donate to the Quilt Show," shares quilt artist Janet M. Tetzlaff.

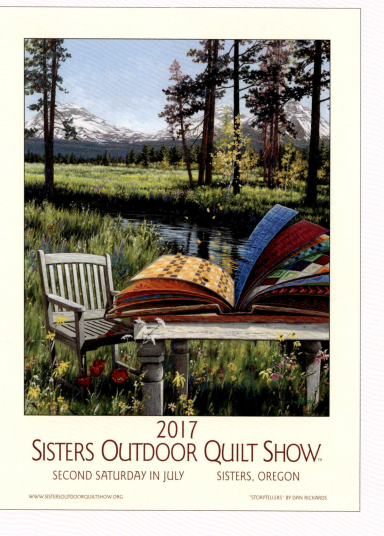

Official 2017 poster, *Storytellers*, by artist Dan Rickards.

The Storybook open to one of my quilts, Color Play.

Dawn M. Boyd shares what attendees can expect when they find the storybook on Quilt Show day: "[The] volunteer Storybook Project hostess will share the story of each quilt to listeners, who are drawn into the correlation between the story and the quilt. Oftentimes, the storytellers will also highlight the special handwork that has gone into the creation of the quilt: the hidden reflection of water stitched into the landscape; the shadowing of the trees among the flowers; the intricate piecing of hand-dyed fabrics. Visitors to the Quilt Show seek out the book and its stories, finding it on Quilt Show day in its recurrent location, the garden area of the Open Door Restaurant, owned by Julie and Dan Rickards. A fitting placement, as it reflects Dan's ongoing commitment to the Quilt Show."

"When we think about the influencers in the quilting industry, Jean Wells is at the top of our list. I will never forget when she came to our booth at one of our first Quilt Markets and placed an order for some Sew Kind of Wonderful products. We were tickled pink! She has been an inspiration to us with her quilting knowledge and creativity. She is always supportive, innovative, creative, and encouraging. She truly has a gift and is one of our favorite people in the quilting world."—Jenny Pedigo and Helen Robinson, designers and instructors

Official 2018 poster, *Creative Trails*, by Paul Alan Bennett.

Sisters, Oregon—Five Decades of Quilting in America

In 2019, having added a number of new features and having seen the Quilt Show through its 40th anniversary, Jeanette retired as executive director and Dawn M. Boyd was hired as the new leader.

That year was Dawn's first Quilt Show to put on, but she came in ready to keep the momentum rolling forward. She had a wonderful friend group, "The Diamonds," from where she used to live, all of whom came to Sisters that year to support Dawn and became a wonderful addition to the army of Quilt Show volunteers.

"The Diamonds" volunteer group, come to join executive Dawn M. Boyd to admire quilts created by the East of the Cascades Quilt Guild.

Dawn and Valori worked together to create a Celebrity Sew Down, their annual fundraiser to support the show during one evening of Quilter's Affair. The Celebrity Sew Down in 2019 was Team Tula Pink versus Team Rob Appell. Each team chose stitchers and set up on the big stage at the high school. Fun was had by all as each group created a quilt. There were door prizes and lots of surprises that evening.

Official 2019 poster, *Bountiful Living*, by Kathy Deggendorfer.

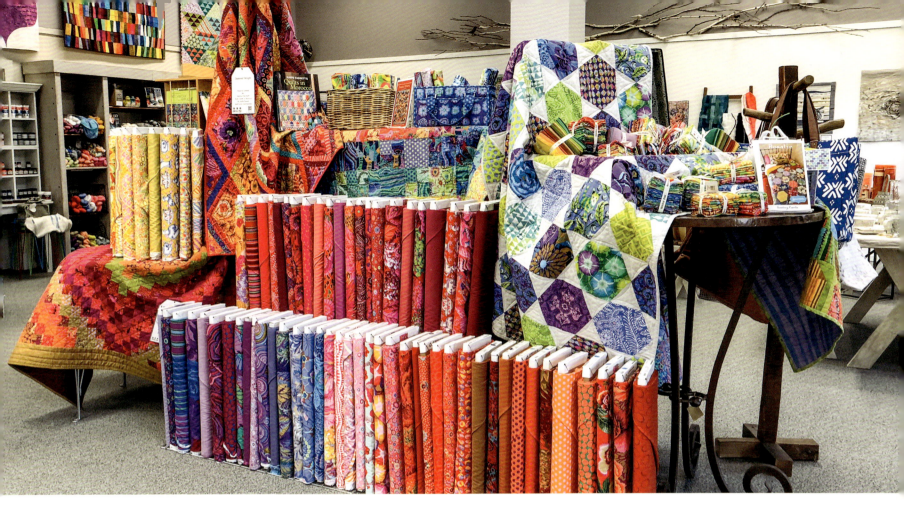

When Plans Change

Like everywhere else in the country, the COVID-19 pandemic hit Central Oregon hard. Valori recalls, "When the COVID shutdown hit the Stitchin' Post, I immediately furloughed all twenty of our employees. My thirteen- and fifteen-year-old daughters and I, along with my retired mother, Jean, set up a system where customers could call in orders and we either mailed them or they could pick them up at the back door. Within a week, I realized that I needed to bring back four key employees to create more newsletters, help with shipping, and create more products out of goods we had in stock to sell. We immediately started putting mask kits together and I spent hours at home making bias ties for the kits.

"Jean started working on educational content that we could use online. I learned how to film and edit videos and our online education programs were launched and still exist today. We filmed tours of the shop to share what we were up to. We applied for one of the early Paycheck Protection Program grants and had the money in our savings account within the week.

"My biggest goal was to stay connected with our people and to create kits to sell and find new items that people could make at home. The floor staff was brought back as we were slowly allowed to open our doors to the public. Weekly newsletter planning sessions were established to keep up with the increased online sales, and [they] still exist today."

Valori put her bachelor's degree in photography to work during the pandemic, sharing images inside and outside of the Stitchin' Post online, keeping us connected in such a magical way. The practice she started photographing our kit quilts outside in different natural settings was a trendsetter online and still exists today.

Valori continues "With July fast approaching, we realized that we needed to pivot for Quilter's Affair. It was impossible to have in-person classes, but we wanted to stay in touch, so our employees pitched in, and I hung twelve different groups of quilts from Monday through Saturday on our building. I filmed these mini shows and talked about the quilt artistry and uploaded them. Our store is located on a major highway in Oregon, so the motorists were entertained, as well as our online audience.

"The COVID experience helped us as a business to reevaluate our customers' needs, as well as gain new online customers who have become loyal to the Stitchin' Post. We have continued to create online classes and YouTube videos that educate and inspire our customers."

The shop and the educational program were not the only things affected. Executive Director Dawn M. Boyd shares, "In March of 2020, we thought there would be a two-week hiatus of meetings in order to stop the spread of COVID-19. By mid-April, we knew it was time to have a board meeting to chat about the possibility of not having an in-person Quilt Show for the first time in 45 years. Our biggest challenge was the commitment to staying connected in a time when we weren't allowed to be together.

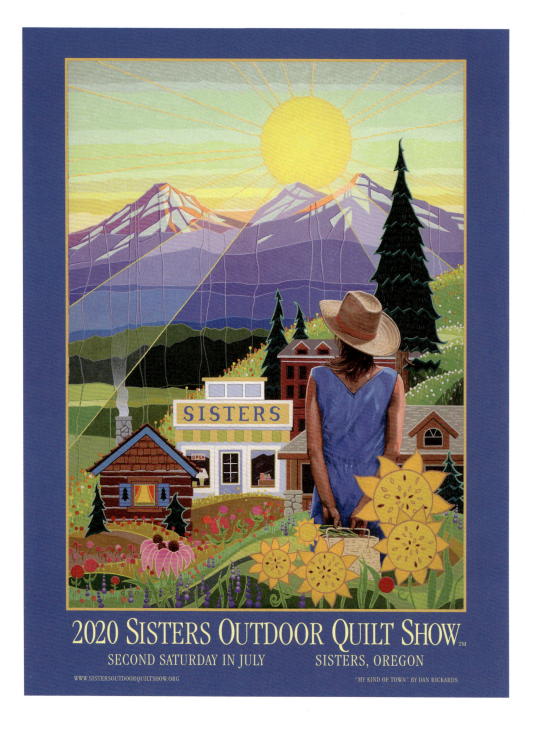

TOP • Official 2020 poster, *My Kind of Town*, by Dan Rickards.

RIGHT • Granddaugher Oliva cuts fabric to fulfill and online order.

Quilts by Tonye B. Phillips, featured quilter of 2020, displayed at her home during the COVID-19 pandemic.

QUILTS LEFT TO RIGHT • *For the Birds, Round Robin, Pavers and Pomegranates,* and *Garden Girls and Greenhouses*

"It was time to think outside the box. Our board began having virtual board meetings, using technology to our advantage, and talking about all of the components that are part of our quilt show. How would we stay connected and share quilts? How could we use additional technology to our advantage?

"Working in collaboration with the City of Sisters, local businesses, our technology crew, and our quilters, we established a new game plan. We were able to pivot and create a virtual Sisters Outdoor Quilt Show. We pre-filmed our special exhibits on local sponsor business buildings, as they would have hung on Quilt Show day. We traveled to the homes of

our featured quilters to showcase their collections of quilts online. And we encouraged all quilters to hang their own quilts somewhere outdoors on Quilt Show day, post on social media, and tag the Sisters Outdoor Quilt Show so that we could share their quilts via our accounts.

"With posting our virtual exhibits on the website and including live feeds highlighting our sponsor businesses, our website and Facebook live videos hit more than 168,000 views on Quilt Show day. The success of our 2020 virtual show was a step forward in expanding our audience to around the world. We now continue this addition to our quilt show in order to not only broaden our audience but continue the tradition of connection through celebrating quilts. The show is now so iconic that it is a bucket-list item for so many quilters.

"Creat[ing] a community and a sense of community when it was needed most, keeping the shop and the show alive, creat[ing] a sense of optimism and community even though not being able to connect in person, … and connection of this online community is now part of the show and is global—hang your quilt in your own yard. Growing globally and virtually engaging in the international quilt community pushed the Stitchin' Post and the Quilt Show to grow into what they are today."—Dawn M. Boyd, Executive Director

Recalling the impact the shop had on her life during the pandemic, Liz Deck, customer and friend of 47 years, recalls that "During the … COVID pandemic, it was the Stitchin' Post that saved my sanity. Being isolated and staying at home was dismal and sad.

"I distinctly remember the day I found Jean on YouTube (or possibly Zoom). The familiarity of her voice, with her smile and happy, unfaltering words of encouragement, caused me to immediately burst into tears of joy and relief. This happened many times for months.

"Her presentations provided a sense of normalcy with sparks and prompts that kept my creative self alive! The ability to shop online that Valori has created was also so important.

"I am so very appreciative of [Jean's] time, and sharing her down-to-earth and can-do attitude. She will always remain a refreshing tonic for myself and my family."

Official 2021 poster, *Renewal*, by Donna Rice.

LEFT • Volunteer Betty Dagget hanging a Face Quilt by Freddy Moran.

RIGHT • Quilts by the Tentmakers of Cairo.

"During the winter of 2021, we had made all of our plans for a traditional Quilt Show, but we were all still in the 'in-between' mode of COVID regulations. By March of 2021, we were still unable to receive confirmation of being able to produce a full-size show. We opted to be proactive and propose a half-size show for approval from the collaborating entities: the Deschutes County Health Department, the City of Sisters, the Fire District, and Sheriff's Department. While we could never give a specific number of guests, we could reduce the number of quilts on view to half, we could notify potential visitors that we would only be at half-capacity, and we could continue the virtual show component to allow those unable or unwilling to travel to stay connected.

"Our day was successful and, indeed, kept visitors and virtual visitors alike connected.

"The hybrid model of 2021 showed once again that the resiliency and think-outside-the-box mentality behind the Quilt Show meant that we would never stay stagnant due to believing everything had to be done the way we had always done them," shares Executive Director Dawn M. Boyd.

The 2021 theme was "Renewal," and for good reason. The featured quilts for this show were made by the Egyptian Tentmakers of Cairo. In Cairo, the Street of the Tentmakers winds its way back into the mists of time. This quilting originated in the Bedouin tribes and has always been done by men. In their Cairo market, stitchers operate out of tiny stalls that have, for centuries, produced exquisite and intricate designs backed by canvas panels. Traditionally, these panels made up the sometimes massive tents of desert Arabs and Ottoman sultans. Today the panels are sold as wall hangings, and several hung in the show and were for sale.

TOP • Quilt sales help support the Tentmakers and their families.

MIDDLE • Traditional, one-block, and unique designs hang side by side. Left to right are *Zesty Vibrance* by Vickie Crockett, *Savannah* by Candy Woods, and *Phases* by Dawn Anderson.

RIGHT • Quilts from the Central Oregon Modern Quilt Guild.

I had met the Tentmakers of Cairo in California when I was teaching a workshop. I had time to visit with them and hear them tell their story to a group of quilters, and I could hardly wait to tell Dawn and Valori about them. They were excited, too, and we worked together to put travel plans in place and plan events for them while they were in Sisters. They like to be able to sell their quilts, as these sales support the artists and their families back in Egypt. We had plans for a lecture and appliqué demonstrations to pass on their methods of stitching. But then came COVID! We had to regroup on short notice. They asked if they would still be able to mail quilts to us to be displayed and made available for sale, and we said yes.

Just visualize when four large boxes arrived at the Stitchin' Post from Egypt. We started to open them and quickly thought about Jim Cornelius, the editor from our local newspaper, *The Nugget*. He came right over with his camera, and we opened the boxes. They were bursting with color and beautiful hand-appliquéd motifs, and we treasured the beauty of the appliqué art. Show attendees purchased most of the pieces, and we were able to send the Tentmakers a nice check.

Our 2024 Quilt Show was defined by very high temperatures, but that did not dampen the spirits of the attendees. Armed with water bottles and sunscreen, the more than 1,000 quilts on display were taken in by thousands.

One of our new components in 2024 was a new partnership with the Rotary Club of Sisters. The Rotary coordinated with local businesses on a new passport program. The purpose of the program is to encourage visitors to visit various businesses in town to get stamps in their Quilt Week Passport for a chance to win a quilt made by Valori and me. This partnership reflects the community connection that is so important to the Quilt Show, bringing local businesses, community service groups, and our attendees together. In addition to this fun activity for Quilt Show week attendees, the Rotary Club fielded a team of volunteers to help hang quilts the morning of the show.

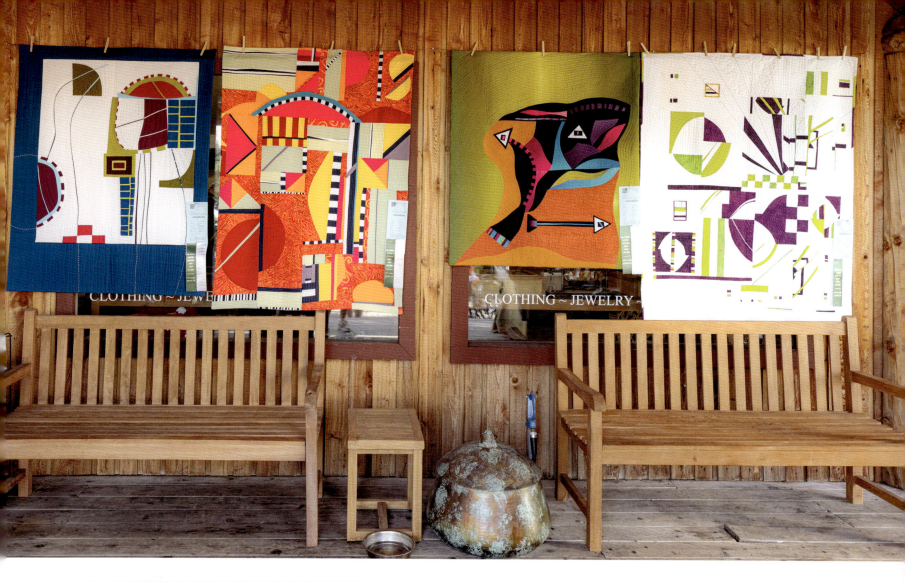

TOP • Left to right, quilts created by Leah Pahlmeyer, Bobbie Gideon, Kumi Fisher, and Diane Jacquith in an Irene Roderick workshop at the Stitchin' Post.

LEFT • Visitors stroll through the Teacher's Pavillion, enjoying quilts made by the Quilter's Affair instructors.

RIGHT • Official 2022 poster, *Creating Community*, textile art by Janet MacConnell.

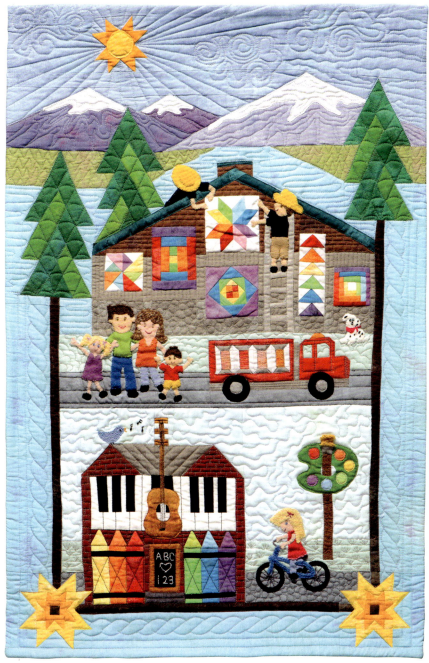

Community

Without the support of our community, the Quilt Show would not have thrived.

Ten years ago, the economic impact of Quilter's Affair and the Sisters Outdoor Quilt Show was $3.2 million. In 2024 dollars, that would be $4.7 million. Folks who come to the show stay in Redmond, Bend, Sisters, and other surrounding communities. The Quilt Show could never have grown to be what it is today without its surrounding community. Our local citizens have, from day one, stepped up to pitch in; in return, the show has found ways to give back, whether it is bringing visitors to town to patronize businesses, introducing locals to the wider world of quilting, or opening up opportunities to fundraise. There is an almost symbiotic relationship between the community and the show, all nestled in one of the more beautiful places in the country.

The U.S. Census Bureau estimated that, in 1977, just two years after the opening of the Stitchin' Post and the first show, the population of Sisters was 827. In 2020, the most recent year for which numbers are available, it estimates the town to have grown to 3,064 people. Clearly the town has grown apace with the show.

The Businesses

"As the Quilt Show has grown over the years, it has become apparent that there is a positive economic impact for not only the city of Sisters, but all of Central Oregon. In 2009, it was estimated that 96 percent of attendees were from out of the Sisters area, and the expenditure estimate for economic impact was $3.2 million. Multiply that number by today's economic inflation, and the impact is much stronger. Providing an event that is free to attend for all, but not free to produce, the Quilt Show relies on its partner sponsor businesses to continue their support of this widely attended event, knowing that it brings a positive impact to our community in such a large way," explains Dawn M. Boyd, Executive Director.

TOP LEFT • *Solarium* was created by Sisters resident Linda Weick using the Riverwalk fabric I designed. Wychus Creek flows through Sisters and was the perfect setting for this quilt.

RIGHT • Visitors come from around the world to share in our love of quilting.

Dawn notes that "A large part of the success of [the] Quilt Show has been the support of many community organizations in partnership and volunteer roles. For many years, the Kiwanis Club of Sisters has provided hanging team volunteers, waking up at the crack of dawn on Quilt Show morning. They arrive ready with their ladders and happy smiles to hang quilts in their section of town. They have been part of this for so long, it is now the next generation of Kiwanians who are leading the pack of volunteers.

"The Sisters Rotary Club has partnered with the Quilt Show in both volunteering and creating fundraising opportunities to benefit both groups. Sisters Community Church provides volunteers and support for the Quilt Show's Holiday Fundraiser. And Sisters Lutheran Church has provided its lawn space for tour bus parking for many years.

"In 2024, Valori and Dawn became charter members of the new Sisters Business Association. They shared with the members what the Quilter's Affair and Quilt Show are about so they could join us in welcoming all the quilters and their friends.

"Working with the City of Sisters, the Oregon Department of Transportation, the Sisters-Camp Sherman Fire District, and the Deschutes County Sheriff's Office, we often see the best of collaboration for success on the day of Quilt Show. One of the more visible roles played is that of our [Sheriff's

LEFT • Quilters travel from all corners of the world to attend the show.

TOP AND RIGHT • Summer in the high desert is hot and the quilts do double duty by providing much needed shade.

deputies serving] crossing-guard duty on show day. Each of these deputies has a smile on their face and a most welcoming attitude to each visitor who is looking to get safely across our busy Cascade Avenue. Chatting with visitors from around the world, our [Sheriff's department plays] a vital role in the success of Quilt Show day."

"Congratulations to the Sisters Outdoor Quilt Show for 50 years of quilting success! The Sisters-Camp Sherman Fire District has been honored to support your efforts to transform Sisters into a global quilting destination. Our firefighters and EMTs love working with the countless volunteers and visitors as they envelope the community admiring the handmade quilts. The SOQS is truly a remarkable community event that the fire district looks forward to every year!"—Roger Johnson, Fire Chief

LEFT • Sisters-Camp Sherman volunteer firemen hanging employee-made quilts on the side of the Stitchin' Post, early on the morning of the Quilt Show

RIGHT • Volunteer firemen hanging *Creative Trails* by Paige Vitek.

"Sisters-Camp Sherman Firefighters may not be quilters, but they are essential to the Sisters Outdoor Quilt Show. They always draw a crowd when carefully hanging staff quilts on the outside of the Stitchin' Post. I enjoy watching the building unfold with color, design, and inspiration. The crew is adept at climbing ladders, hoisting precious quilts and following specific directions. For over twenty years now, they have listened to my instructions. They only give me one do-over. I have great memories working with these men and women. I remember the fire whistle going off right in the middle of our work. I will not forget the honorary child's fire hat they made me wear while riding in the fire truck when our work was done."—Sally Frey, Quilter's Affair instructor and volunteer

Sisters, Oregon—Five Decades of Quilting in America

LEFT • Many businesses and restaurants in Sisters are must-visit destinations for Quilt Show attendees.

RIGHT • Special exhibit of quilts made by Irene Roderick students in a 2023 Stitchin' Post workshop, displayed on the front porch of Bedouin.

Dawn continues to explain that, whether it is the fire district offering first aid, hanging quilts, and selling hot dogs, or local kids selling water bottles to raise funds for their dance or sports teams, it is truly a community-focused event. "One of the most important factors of the Sisters Outdoor Quilt Show is knowing that when we focus on connecting with our community, we all succeed, and then the community of Sisters will continue to succeed."

When we undertook to set the story of our Quilt Show down on paper, we reached out to our local community to ask how the show has affected them as a community, as businesses, and personally. So many were generous with their responses.

"Alongside the incredible financial impact of the Quilt Show, I personally look forward to curating the store every year for the special day.

"I love when the day finally comes, we open early, and I appreciate seeing everyone's enthusiasm for others' work and the creative energy is flowing."—Harmony Thomas, owner of Bedouin, a local boutique clothing store

"For 50 years the Sisters Outdoor Quilt Show has brought together multiple generations of quilters to our community. The result is a flurry of colors, patterns, and geometric shapes hung from every corner of every business; no space is left untouched. The Quilt Show, for one brief day a year, alters the character of our town. It reminds us of beauty, tradition, and what community means. Here's to another 50 years!"—Spencer Hamiga, owner of Sisters Bakery

"My grandparents, Robert and Claudia Grooney, have been part of the Quilt Show since my childhood. I used to run around the Gallimaufry [gift shop] and all over town looking at all the quilts, marveling at how our town got transformed into a sea of people from all over the world. It was always the single most important sales day of the year, which took a lot of preparation. We would employ all family members for that day, and at day's end, everyone would be exhausted and telling stories of the day over dinner. You could say it was a kind of local holiday in our house.

"I am carrying on my grandparents' legacy by running the Gallimaufry and the Sisters Liquor Store. Even though the COVID-19 pandemic really took a toll on events in Sisters, they have come back.

"By adapting to the times, I'm excited to see how the Quilt Show is evolving by honoring its history at the same time [as it is] welcoming new blood and incorporating modern visions. I'm looking forward to my kids gaining an appreciation for the art and [becoming] excited about the energy the show can bring."—Spud Shaw, owner of the Gallimaufry

Spud hanging quilts with his grandfather, Bob Grooney, one of the first people to step forward and help us create teams to hang the quilts.

"The Chicks and Rooster at the Hen's Tooth [gift shop] congratulate SOQS/Stitchin' Post for creating a monumental event that for 50 years has inspired and entertained people from around the world. The atmosphere outdoors in Sisters elevates on Quilt Show day—the excitement is tangible as hundreds of colorful quilts captivate attendees. And indoors, our second-generation mom-and-pop business consistently experiences its best sales day of the year. With gratitude to the multitude of volunteers who make this day possible, we *salute* you!"—Heather Olson.

"The best part for me of my 22-year journey with the Stitchin' Post and with the Quilt Show is being in touch with all of the quilters over the years. (I take care of all the making of packages at the store.) [Whether] it's just sending a caring note to someone working in a war zone in Afghanistan, an email to check on you after a 7.1 earthquake in Alaska, or a caring get-well email to you over in the UK, that is one of the best parts of being involved in this amazing quilting community. And getting to see all of the guests over the years."—Annette Caldwell, purchasing manager, the Stitchin' Post

Official 2023 poster, *Hidden Stories*, by Kelly Ray Roberts.

"The Quilt Show is literally stitched into the history of the city of Sisters. As one of the city's early large-scale events, you have so importantly helped shape what the city is today. Quilt Show attendees have [traveled], and will continue to travel, from all over the world to see the world's largest outdoor quilt show. As mayor, Quilt Show weekend is my favorite each year because I get to meet so many people from different countries and faraway places on the streets and have fun and welcoming conversations. A big thank-you for adorning the city with all of the beautiful quilts across our downtown storefronts. It reminds me of how our city itself is much like a quilt—different people with different backgrounds and different ideas, who live together in this most wonderful community. Thank you Sisters [Outdoor] Quilt Show for being such an important showcase for our town and letting the locals be a part of it.

"I can't wait until we do it again."—Michael Preedin, Mayor, City of Sisters

"Fifty years … there have been a lot of changes in 50 years in Central Oregon. People, businesses, and events have come and gone, but the Sisters Outdoor Quilt Show continues to thrive. I believe it is the spirit of inclusiveness and the honest celebration of the arts that sustains this annual gathering. The Sisters Outdoor Quilt Show has defined our community and transformed Sisters into a place that is known for creativity and kindness. What a legacy!"—Kathy Deggendorfer, 2025 poster artist and founder of the Roundhouse Foundation

TOP • *Two Rivers, Three Sisters* quilt series. From left to right, quilts by Sheila Finzer, Jean Wells & Valori Wells, June Jaeger, Catherine Moen, Janice W. Hearn, Pat Welsh, Mary Stiewig, Sarah Kaufman, Helen Brisson, Betty Gientke, Tonye B. Phillips, Cindy Young, Mary Nyquist Koons, Judy Johnson, Donna Cherry, Carol Webb, and Donna Rice.

LEFT • The quilts change every year and businesses come and go, but at its heart, the show is the same as those first years.

RIGHT • Official 2024 poster, *Dreamscapes*, by Cheryl Chapman.

Drawn into the Art

Ann Richardson, former executive director, explained that in 2011, several quilters from Central Oregon were commissioned by the U.S. Forest Service and the National Forest Foundation to create individual wall quilts to raise money for forest restoration. The quilts depicted Whychus Creek joining the Metolius River. The quilts would hang in a row, connecting one quilt to the next one: *Two Rivers, Three Sisters*. "Donna Rice designed the project and each artist offered her own interpretation of Whychus Creek. It is a 40-foot showcase piece that now hangs in the council room at the Sisters City Hall. This is a stellar representation of community partnerships and what Sisters is all about."

The *Two Rivers, Three Sisters* quilts traveled with me to Yokohama, Japan, where I visited as an artist and lecturer. I was invited to exhibit my quilts at the Yokohama International Quilt Show. The quilts were the very first exhibit you saw when you entered the show! I was so proud of the *Two Rivers* quilts being shown in this prestigious show.

"I joined staff at the Sisters Public Library, Fall 2005, making this my nineteenth year to carry on the tradition of library participation. It's wonderful experiencing all the creativity and camaraderie of those in the quilting world, as well as meeting those attendees who join us in the library during the weeks leading up to and after the show. My staff and I look forward to the event every year!

"At one point, I had someone share with me, 'Within the quilting community, a trip to the Sisters Outdoor Quilt Show is the equivalent of a trip to Disneyland. Some folks save for years to make this happen.' When we found ourselves in the throes of the pandemic summer 2020, your team pivoted successfully to a virtual platform, so the show went on. Since that time, you [have continued] to integrate some of those platforms, thus opening up the opportunity for many to participate ... literally thousands more."—Zoe Schumacher, Sisters Public Library

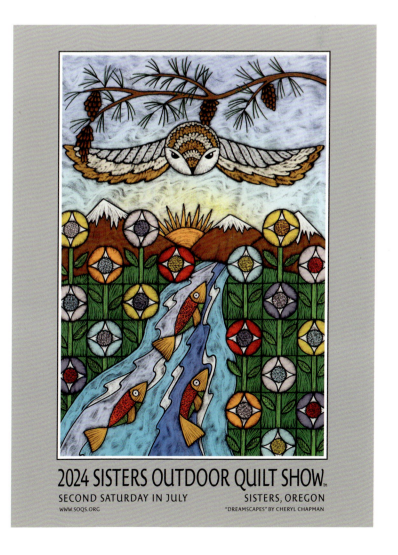

Log Cabin quilt by Jackie Erickson

Finding Community

"Someone asked me the other day, what I thought community was. August 4, 2010 changed my life and introduced me to a wonderful community that I had belonged to for a very long time but had not realized it.

"A wildfire near Sisters broke out along Whychus Creek on August 10, 2010. The path the fire took led directly to an outbuilding that held all of my family's possessions as we were in the middle of a move to a new home. Needless to say, the building was destroyed along with everything we owned inside. As devastating as the situation was, there was a silver lining: my quilting community.

"As soon as quilters and friends heard about the fire, they came together and supported my family and me. I had met many of these wonderful women and men through the Stitchin' Post, Quilters Affair, and Quilt Show.

"Letters and cards poured in. Some sent fabric to start my new stash with. Some sent quilts and quilt tops. Some even sent quilts that I had gifted them in the past! And some sent money to get us back on our feet. One wonderful quilter even gifted me with a new Bernina sewing machine! She stipulated that I must continue to make charity quilts, and I have. A true outpouring of love and support from people I knew and many I had never met before.

"But the quilting community is just that. A group of friends and friends we haven't met yet. Men and women who care about each other's well-being. We celebrate our victories, indulge in our famil[ies] and friends. Come together in sorrow. Lean on each other when we need comfort. The quilting community is vast and encompasses the entire world. If you are reading this, you are part of this amazing community," shares Jackie Erickson, longtime Sisters resident and employee and instructor at the Stitchin' Post.

Through the Sponsor Quilt Program, supporting businesses are provided with a quilt, made by an Oregon quilter, to be hung in their business for the month of July. In turn, we advertise the location of each sponsor quilt in our Quilt Walk brochure, which provides the businesses with foot traffic. Quilt Walk participants get to see some great quilts at their own pace and are introduced to new local businesses.

Helen Brisson notes that "With so many quilters in town the week before the show and after, we like to highlight our local businesses that so graciously help to promote this amazing show.

"As sponsor coordinator, I visit each business to determine where and what will fit with not only the décor of the business, but the type of business.

"The joy on the faces of the business owners and employees when the quilt is delivered is always over the top.

"We could not do this without the support of all quilters. Putting a call out for specific themes is always met with great response from all of our quilters, some new, some long time."

Must Visits

Whether you are planning your first visit to Sisters or your 50th, there is always something new to explore in the greater area. When you find yourself with a little bit of downtime, why not check out one of these incredible spots?

The High Desert Museum, located just south of Bend, Oregon, features wildlife and art exhibits that will engage you in the cultural and natural history of Central Oregon.

Camp Sherman, famous for its fly-fishing, is a tiny community west of Sisters, near the Metolius River. It boasts a charming country store and plentiful walking trails.

Three Creek Lake is a picturesque mountain lake located at the base of Broken Top Mountain. To get there, follow Ash Street south out of Sisters toward the Three Sisters Mountains.

The **Tam McArthur Rim Trail** in the Deschutes National Forest is a very popular day hike. The trailhead is located on the northeastern shore of the lake. Self-issued wilderness permits are required and can be obtained at recreation.gov.

Smith Rock State Park offers scenic views of the Crooked River Canyon and is considered the birthplace of modern rock climbing. Located just north of Redmond, near Terrebonne, Oregon, the park boasts several thousand climbs.

Dee Wright Observatory is a Civilian Conservation Corps structure in the Willamette National Forest, completed in 1935. From this lava stone building, located in the midst of a large lava flow at the summit of the McKenzie Pass, you get amazing views of a number of Cascade peaks. Follow Highway 242 west out of Sisters to the summit of the McKenzie Pass.

Hoodoo Ski Area is a winter ski area and summer recreation mecca for hiking and water sports just west of Sisters. The Pacific Crest Trail runs through the area.

Whychus Creek Overlook offers bold and scenic views of the Whychus Creek Wild and Scenic River area and the peaks of the Three Sisters mountains. Follow Ash Street south out of Sisters to find the trailhead. Hike the one-mile accessible trail to the clifftop overlook.

To find out even more about our community and what is happening, be sure to pick up the weekly *The Nugget* newspaper in town and a visitor's guide at the Sisters Visitors Center or at sistersoregonguide.com.

Two of my quilts, hung on the front of the Stitchin' Post, reflect the local attractions.

The Volunteers

"When I came on board as executive director in 2019, I had been told to not worry—volunteers would help the show happen," explains Dawn M. Boyd, Executive Director. "Little did I understand the depth of every little component of [the] show production would indeed be due to the help of over 300 amazing people. Not only is my life richer due to the help that all of these volunteers give (both brand-new each year, and those who return year after year), but for the many who have become friends."

Dawn further explains that the Sisters Outdoor Quilt Show is truly remarkable in that, for an event its size, it has a minimal staff but a multitude of volunteers who give so many hours to its success. "Our volunteers are from not only Sisters and Central Oregon, but from across the country. I believe that there is an understanding of what the Quilt Show and Quilter's Affair brings to the quilting world: a chance to see work up close and personal by some of your favorite world-renown[ed] teachers, a chance to commiserate with quilters and quilting fans of every similitude, and a chance to give back to the world of quilting by helping with the SOQS volunteer opportunities. This is part of what makes our quilt show a continuing success."

Our day of sharing couldn't happen without an army of volunteers.

The Undercover Quilters from Bend, Oregon, exhibit, 2024. This guild selects a book each year to read and discuss, and then each member creates a quilt.

Former Executive Director Jeanette Pilak notes that "Fifty years of celebrating creativity and the wonders of quilting arts is phenomenal. When I arrived for the 39th anniversary, I was attracted because of the economic impact an event could have on the town where I lived. But that barely scratched the surface of the phenomenon that is the Sisters Outdoor Quilt Show.

"The impacts of the creative inspiration enjoyed by quilters and non-quilters alike are immeasurable. That a first-time quilter can hang their work next to a world-renowned quilter is, frankly, brilliant and unheard of. The transformation of a small, rural town into an international mecca of friends, visitors, creatives, and quilters is unmatched. The depth of volunteerism among locals, and those who come from afar to work hard, makes the impossible one-day show a magical reality. Local business owners pitch in with ideas that fertilize the diverse aspects of this creative endeavor to keep it growing. Friendships sparked over color, fabric, creativity—or just standing next to each other experiencing a quilt together—endure for lifetimes.

"Some say Jean Wells hanging twelve quilts outside in 1975 is 'humble beginnings.' I choose to believe it is her unlimited well of creative, positive thinking that continues to inspire and create phenomenal art for and with the world."

"The quilt show is a joyous time of year where little elves hang the quilts [on] the buildings with care, in preparation for a long summer day. Where happy people wander among the wondrous delights, where the merchants see inventory flying off the shelves, and eateries are just packed. The whole show is like a box of chocolates, the visitors never know what they will see next. An adventure in wonderland. That's why they come from all over the world to see the show."—Michael Denton, longarm quilter and quiltmaker showing his work at the show

Christine Shimizu shares that "Every year, I volunteer in the show office to give back to the community, as well as support my quilt-minded friends. It's no surprise that I always benefit more than I give. The excitement throughout the town is palpable. I feel that each show offers inspiration, creativity, friendship, and laughter to all who join in the fun."

Many volunteers return year after year to help hang quilts throughout town.

"*Over 21 years ago, my husband and I were on a trip through Oregon from Massachusetts. One must stop was at the Stitchin' Post, when I had 30 minutes to shop before heading to our next destinations. That one stop has led to moving to Bend, many classes and opportunities that have developed my art and joy, and volunteering and participating as a quilter at the Quilt Show. Volunteering, for me, has offered great insight of the vibes of the show, the visitors, the buzz of activity, and of course, the wonderful, colorful, special quilts! That legacy of a handful of quilts hung outside Jean's shop 50 years ago continues to evolve into the invaluable vision of what has led so many to enjoy this event.*" —Martha Phair Sanders

Diane Tolzman also recalls being a part of the show for many years, starting as a visitor, then as a volunteer, and finally getting the courage to submit a quilt. "It has also been a way for me to teach my three grandkids to quilt and for them to experience the pride and joy of seeing your quilt on the streets of Sisters!"

It's no wonder that so many people volunteer, and do so year after year. "Our first visit to the Sisters Outdoor Quilt Show in the late 1990s was magical—a colorful, joyful experience in a friendly environment. In subsequent years, I began taking Quilter's Affair classes the week before the Quilt Show and volunteered, starting with folding quilts, for the Quilt Show. This introduced me to a community of quilters and the community of Sisters. Volunteering for the Quilt Show has provided me the opportunity to make friendships and work with others dedicated to making the show a wonderful celebration of quilting and fiber arts. I enjoy having my quilts shown in this unique outdoor show that captivated my imagination so long ago, and I am grateful to be able to contribute to the production of the show through volunteering," recalls Marion Shimoda, volunteer and board member.

Volunteers contribute more than 900 hours before, during, and after the show.

Sisters, Oregon—Five Decades of Quilting in America

Part of the beauty of the growth of our quilt show is that it now takes more than 300 volunteers to make things happen, and they contribute more than 900 hours before, during, and after the show.

Some volunteers are behind the scenes, doing myriad jobs that make sense once you know everything it takes to make the show happen. It takes all these jobs to contribute to the success of the show, and is the secret to taking care of the more than 1,000 quilts that have been entrusted to us.

A key component to that care is our Quilt Rescue Team. If you can envision the Lone Ranger, riding up on his horse ready to save the day, that is our Quilt Rescue Team. They are equipped to handle any quilt rescue they might be called to. With golf carts primed and ready to go and ladders and clothespins on hand, the Quilt Rescue Team saves quilts that have been caught by the wind or have started to loosen. They are also ready to repair any loose wire, deliver show guides to a needy information booth, or just point a guest to a specific special exhibit or even the nearest ATM. And while these particular volunteers aren't truly behind the scenes, they certainly ensure that our Quilt Show day is one of successful fun for everyone!

LEFT • Quilt Rescue Team volunteers Ross Kennedy and Eric Spencer, ready to handle any emergency.

RIGHT • Rehanging quilts that have come loose is a key job for any Quilt Rescue Team member.

The Quilt Show Gives Back

As a thriving nonprofit, the Quilt Show maintains its mission: to celebrate the art, skill, and heritage of quilting and fiber arts, while enhancing the cultural vitality of Sisters and Central Oregon and providing enrichment opportunities for area youth.

Carol Dixon, board member, notes that the show has close ties with the Sisters school community. "Through the Graduate Resource Organization program at Sisters High School, SOQS provides a yearly $1,000 scholarship to a deserving Sisters High School graduating senior. Known as the SOQS Arts and Design Enrichment Scholarship, the qualifications are as follows: 'To recognize and honor a graduating Sisters High School senior who desires to pursue college classes as enrichment in the area of art and/or design perhaps but not necessarily leading to an art/design or business degree.' Funds for the scholarship are raised through the Quilt Show WISH Card program. (page 159).

"Other areas of Sisters schools connections include fundraising opportunities for various school groups. The district's music department runs a successful quilters' bed-and-breakfast (called School House B&B) at the Sisters Middle School campus during the week of Quilter's Affair … [and] volleyball players help out quilters by carrying their heavy sewing machines for them. The Jazz Dance Team helps on Quilt Show day with myriad needs surrounding setting up for the show. All of these opportunities and activities provide vital links with our younger Sisters community."

Imagine how surprised I was to receive the prestigious Ben Westlund Memorial Award from the Deschutes Cultural Coalition of the Oregon Cultural Trust in 2020. "The honor is awarded to those who have served tirelessly throughout the years to forward arts and culture in Central Oregon," according to Cate O'Hagan. It was really special to be honored as the founder of the Sisters Outdoor Quilt Show and for my continued involvement in it. The joy that the hanging of non-juried quilts in our beautiful mountain community brings to everyone is my gift to Sisters.

The interconnected and interdependent relationship between our community, the Stitchin' Post, the annual show, and the art and craft of quilting itself is summed up best by Jim Cornelius, editor in chief of *The Nugget* newspaper and cofounder of the Sisters Folk Festival. "Quilting is, to me, like folk music—a traditional art form of the people that evolves in endless new directions, bringing together diverse cultural influences, yet always reflecting the heart and soul of the creator. The Sisters Outdoor Quilt Show celebrates the dynamism of quilting and the fabric arts—and celebration is the right word. In covering the SOQS for *The Nugget* Newspaper, I always come away from interviews invigorated and inspired by the pure joy in creativity shared by all the participants, from established artists to spectators. SOQS has been inspiring people for half a century—a remarkable accomplishment that's worthy of celebration in its own right."

Piles of scraps await workshop participants.

the Quilts

Morning Sun, *by Jean Wells.*

LEFT • In 2017, pink was the theme for the quilts hung on the front of the Stitchin' Post.

RIGHT • It's important that the quilts fit the location, as well as work well with the quilts hung nearby.

If you aren't familiar with quilt competitions, jurying is the selection process by which a quilt is admitted into a show, and judging is the process by which awards are given to select quilts. Ours is a grassroots show with no judging or jurying. Our show invites beginning quilters, as well as accomplished ones. It is not uncommon to see a newly minted quilter at the show with their extended family sharing the story of their quilt and to see famous quilters mingling with everyone.

From the very beginning, the show has been open to everyone. A wide variety of styles are represented, from someone's very first patchwork quilt to a prize-winning art quilt. It is magical! Quilters are storytellers with their craft, which is evident when you stroll through Sisters the second Saturday in July. Magical stories are shared, techniques are explored, and beautiful stitching is admired.

TOP LEFT • The Quilt Show continues to be a day of sharing, even 50 years later.

TOP RIGHT • On Quilt Show day the inside of the Stitchin' Post can be as busy as the town itself.

BOTTOM RIGHT • On the left is the quilt made by Takai Onoyama's quilt group for my son, Jason, and me.

The idea behind the very first show was to be a day of sharing, and nothing has changed over the past 50 years.

Over the years, so many special groups and people have shared their work and talent with the community of Sisters and show visitors alike. In 1988, I met Takai Onoyama, a Japanese shop owner, while attending the annual Quilt Market industry trade show. I invited her to display Japanese quilts at the annual quilt show, and she sent thirteen quilts to be showcased. Takai's mini group of quilters in Japan made a quilt for myself and my son who was serving in the Army during the Gulf War.

Sometimes, quilters and guilds shared truly unique creations. In 2009, the Santiam Scrappers Quilt Guild of Lebanon and Karen Wells of Jefferson Threadheads brought two quilted cars, cars actually covered in fabric quilt blocks, to share at the show.

Sharing sometimes flowed outward from Sisters. When my oldest grandson was in the first grade in Portland, I traveled up to his classroom twice a month to work with the students on a math exercise. The project tasked students to work with geometric shapes to create designs that resembled quilt blocks. Students began by arranging shapes and coloring them on paper. Next, I brought precut solid-colored fabric shapes for each child to play with and create designs on a flannel board. I then demonstrated stitching some of them together on my sewing machine in the classroom so the children could watch and took the rest home. Jackie Erickson helped me piece the rest of them and assemble the blocks into a quilt. When I returned with the quilt, they all got to enjoy it!

Local quilter Barbara Myers Fortman reminisces that her mother, Joanne Myers, from Bend, Oregon, was a prolific quilter and fond of rescuing quilts. After hand-quilting a *Crown of Flowers* quilt for a customer, she made several of her own versions of this antique quilt design. Joanne's quilting ability amazed and influenced her three daughters. Debbie Myers, her oldest, began quilting in 1990 and entered quilts in the show. Jamie Forsythe, her second daughter, made whimsical quilted vests. Barbara, Joanne's third daughter, has relocated to Bend and is very active in the Mt. Bachelor and Modern Quilt Guilds. "I always enjoyed being an admirer of quilts until I retired in 2015," Barbara says. "The 'bug' caught me and now I am as prodigious a quilter as my mother was."

LEFT • Braden Wells with quilt made by his first-grade classmates and him.

RIGHT • *Crown of Flowers* quilt made by Joanne Myers.

LEFT • Quilts by friends LeeAnn Decker and Tina N. Davis hanging side by side. Left is *Feedsack Stars and Vines*, created by LeeAnn, quilted by Sharon Tucker; and right is *Salvaged Signatures* by Tina Davis.

RIGHT • Visitors will find quilts hung not just down our main Cascade Avenue, but throughout town. These quilts are by Valori Wells.

Another local quilter, Tina N. Davis, recalls her introduction to the quilt show. "In the early months of 2022, I made a transition from the rainy landscapes of Washington State to the sun-kissed setting of Central Oregon. Little did I anticipate that this relocation would intertwine my story with the Sisters Outdoor Quilt Show, an annual event that had been on [my] periphery until then.

"The excitement among my Washington friends was palpable when they learned I'd be living near Sisters, the hub of SOQS. Plans quickly materialized for the opportunity to explore this renowned event together. Amongst the group was LeeAnn Decker, a friend whose enthusiasm sparked a quilting venture.

"LeeAnn, in her experience, persuaded me to submit my cherished *Salvaged Signatures* quilt for the non-juried show. Despite my initial reservations, her assurance, backed by her own personal quilt entry, convinced me to take the plunge. LeeAnn guided me through the online entry process.

"Since I was now local, I personally delivered my quilt to Sisters, while LeeAnn's creation, *Feedsack Stars and Vines*, embarked on a cross-state journey from Washington. As the online notifications confirmed [the] acceptance of our quilts into the show, the revelation that they would hang together at the same location added an unexpected excitement to the event.

"Unfortunately, LeeAnn had to forgo her trip to Sisters that year. Undeterred, I ventured to the show alone. Amidst the vibrant outdoor display at the Bunkhouse, I discovered my quilt in the company of LeeAnn's hanging not only at the same location but side by side, creating a 'poignant moment of connection.' This serendipitous incident, born of LeeAnn's supportive nudges and my own immersion in the world of quilting, solidified my bond with SOQS and its welcoming community.

"Now, a few years later, I proudly wear the hats of a friend, a volunteer, and a contributor to the Sisters Outdoor Quilt Show. What began as a mere relocation has transformed into a chapter in my life's journey, with SOQS emerging not just as a yearly event but as an integral part of my narrative."

For some quilters, even those who have participated for years, the show can create a spark, which was the case for June Jaeger. "Nine years in the making, *Vision of Horses* emerged. Life had gotten in the way of my creativity. But in my dreams it was still alive as I always woke up visualizing horses running down a hill toward me ... I drew up my own pattern and used Ruth McDowell's curved machine piecing technique to complete my favorite quilt."

For Darlene Wheeler of Idaho, quilting is a family affair. For years, Darlene attended with friends. Then her husband, Chuck, got intrigued and decided to take up quilting. He accompanied Darlene to the Sisters Outdoor Quilt Show and decided he wanted to enter a quilt himself. Their granddaughter Kasey started quilting at age seven, and she's still at it as a freshman in college, part of a family contribution to the iconic show. Truly a grand participation from the Wheeler family, there have been quilts on display from the whole crew: Darlene, Chuck, and now three of their granddaughters. That's the kind of thing that makes SOQS something special and keeps participants coming back for decades.

TOP • *Vision of Horses*, by June Jaeger. Her quilt hung in her featured quilter exhibit in the 2024 show.

RIGHT • Two vibrant quilts provide a pop of color.

One of the favorite special exhibits at the show is the Teacher's Pavillion where the instructors from the Quilter's Affair display some of their work.

Quilters have been exploring the repurposing of fabric since time began, and you can find quilts featuring treasured or repurposed fabrics throughout the show each year. These days, we see some wonderful tributes to meaningful cloth. Marion Shimoda, longtime volunteer and present board member, created *Lei Makers*, a quilt pieced with fabric from two garments block printed and fashioned by Hawaiian artist Allen Akina. "Allen was a young artist in the 1970s when my parents started collecting his artwork and wearing the clothing he designed; he passed away in 1991 at age 51. The middle panel of the quilt came from the back of a shirt my father wore, and the surrounding fabric came from the ruffles on the bottom of a muumuu. Both garments were in disrepair and had been stored for dozens of years. While salvaging the fabric and using it in this piece, I reflected on Allen's artwork, primarily Hawaiian people, that graced the walls of our home, and on Mom and Dad dressed up to go out in their fine clothes designed by Allen. For me, this piece brings to mind the people and gardens of Hawaii."

LEFT (2) • Teacher's Pavilion exhibit of quilts.

RIGHT • *Lei Makers*, by Marion Shimoda.

Sisters, Oregon—Five Decades of Quilting in America

LEFT • Freddy Moran in front of her famous face quilts.

MIDDLE • Some years we nearly had more employee challenge quilts than we had space on the side of our building.

RIGHT • *Parts Department*, by Gwen Marston and Freddy Moran.

"As a novice quilter, being part of the show helped me to see how important my contributions were to the show. I love being near my displayed quilts and hearing what people have to say about [them]. It helps me to better understand what other eyes see in my work. Participating in SOQS makes you feel part of a very special community. Fifty years is just the beginning for all of us."—Jessica W. Burr

Right alongside a maker's first quilt, there could very easily be a quilt by a renowned artist. This can be a big ask from an iconic quilter—enter your quilt in a show that is free to attend and unjuried, that offers no prizes, and we'll be hanging your quilt outdoors to boot! However, year after year, entries pour in from award-winning quilters and popular instructors, all happy to have their work showcased within the wider community of quilters.

"In 1999, I wrote a book, *Freddy's House*, and Jean made a point to meet me as she really liked my book. She told me about this outdoor quilt show she put on in Sisters and suggested I might want to attend. The next summer I made the trip to Sisters with my husband. I vividly remember walking into the old high school to take a workshop at the Quilter's Affair the first time. I was so overwhelmed that a store in Sisters, Oregon, could offer such a variety of classes with nationally known instructors along with talented instructors from Central Oregon. I was hooked! Then on Saturday morning we were amazed to watch the volunteer firemen put up quilts on the east end of the Stitchin' Post that the employees had created.

As the day progressed, I had conversations with complete strangers, and I was hooked on coming back to Sisters again."—Freddy Moran, quilt artist

Later, Freddy Moran met Gwen Marston, well-known art quilter, at the Road to California Quilt Show, and a lasting friendship emerged between these two talented quilters. Freddy invited Gwen to come to her home and she went. They began with a friendship quilt and collaborated on two different books, making quilts to fill all of the pages. They were invited to teach at the Quilter's Affair twice, where they taught separately. Then on Friday night, at the picnic in the park, they gave a joint lecture outside while their quilts were paraded around the tables by my grandchildren and Stitchin' Post employees.

the Educators

A work in progress project from a Quilter's Affair class taught by Sue Spargo.

Though it has grown to a full week of classes boasting dozens of renowned instructors, Quilter's Affair, the educational program of the Sisters Outdoor Quilt Show, started small. June Jaeger remembers "I started teaching at the Sisters Outdoor Quilt Show in 1983. There were only three of us then. I had a small class of twelve students, and we used the classrooms in the old grade school. It was a hot day, and the students sat at these little student desks.

"Shortly after, a new modern middle school was built. At this time, ten to fifteen teachers were invited to teach, some nationally known teachers, and the popular local teachers. We were honored to be a part of this growing tradition. We each had fifteen to twenty students. At this time, the music department teacher organized a bed-and-breakfast program as a fundraiser for the music students. The quilters loved being at the middle school sleeping on cots and being taken care of by the students.

"In the 1990s, the beautiful new Sisters High School was built. It has large classrooms, labs, and a large art room. Quilter's Affair had truly arrived and is now 30 instructors. I have had students from the United Kingdom, Australia, New Zealand, Canada, and Japan, as well as every state in the United States.

"A few years ago, I had a student describe Quilter's Affair like this, 'Traveling in from California to this little, tiny town made me question what I had signed up for. I drove out into the forest, and here was this huge beautiful school tucked in the pines. It was shocking! Lots of white-haired ladies, as well as young people, entering the high school with their supplies. I thought I had entered the *Twilight Zone*.'

"Teaching for over 40 years here at the Quilter's Affair has been an honor."

Longtime quilter Lou Shafer has strong ties to the program and also remembers the early days of the educational event. "The second weekend in July (and then week) was automatically filled in on new calendars! At first Janni, my sister, and I were attendees to experience the Saturday show. Then we attended Mary Ellen Hopkins's delightful lecture and took classes at the grade school. I recall one time students in a class … didn't have supplies so someone dashed off to the Stitchin' Post with their shopping list. I suggested to Jean that perhaps she ought to set up a mini store with special items, 'One more great SP service.' I think it took another year or so before the school shop was established, and my niece so enjoyed staffing that little store for many years. Even though she's not a quilter, she always told everyone she loved hanging out with 'her moms' and other quilters. Her moms certainly enjoyed that, too."

LEFT • Workshops utilize the classrooms at Sisters High School.

RIGHT • As many as 30 instructors gather each year to teach 1,200 students.

Beginning with the first Quilter's Affair in 1980, the educational program has grown to offer a wide variety of workshops from as many as 30 instructors who gather for the five days prior to the show to offer classes at the local high school. While in Sisters, instructors truly become part of the Stitchin' Post family. Over the week of workshops and lectures, instructors from as far away as Australia to as close as down the road interact as a group while they share their techniques and quilting knowledge. The teachers truly become a part of the Quilt Show, as well as sharing some of their masterpiece quilts in the Teacher's Pavillion on the day of the show.

Valori shares her approach to curating this educational experience. "Quilters Affair is a truly magical event. Each year, our local high school transforms into a vibrant hub of fiber arts. Over the course of five days, we offer more than 25 classes daily, fueled by a shared passion for learning and teaching. What makes this event special is not only the diverse range of workshops, but the community's enthusiasm to learn and share knowledge.

"I carefully handpick every instructor to ensure a rich variety of classes centered around quilting and fiber arts. When welcoming a new teacher, I make a point of speaking with them to introduce the event's unique culture and share our journey. Creating a positive, collaborative environment among our teaching staff is essential, as they serve as the ambassadors for both Quilter's Affair and our shop.

"Throughout the week, 1,200 students immerse themselves in classes, expanding their skills, exploring new techniques, and gathering inspiration. The excitement in the air is contagious, and it's impossible not to fall in love with the experience of being part of Quilter's Affair."

The Quilter's Affair is also an opportunity to involve and benefit the community. The Sisters High School volleyball team helps students bring their supplies into the classroom as a fundraiser and the Jazz Dance Team helps with quilt frame placement at the Quilt Show. Several nonprofit groups in Sisters set up booths and provide snacks and beverages for the attendees to raise funds.

The Sisters High School volleyball team helps students bring their sewing machines and supplies into the classroom as a fundraiser.

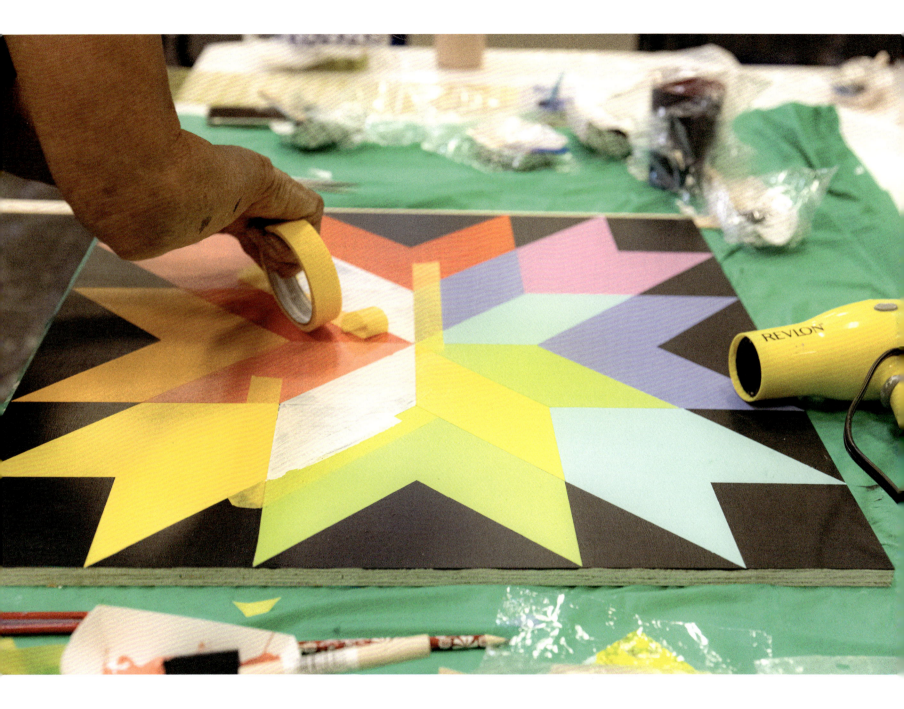

The Stitchin' Post makes every effort to keep the workshop fees affordable for all quilters. Many arrive in their RVs and camp in the campgrounds with their quilting friends. In this casual atmosphere, visitors have the opportunity to meet well-known instructors in person and talk about quilts. It is a magical time for all.

Classes offered at Quilter's Affair are varied and cover more t han quilting.

Classes cover everything from traditional techniques to landscape quilts and much more.

Diane Jaquith, co-coordinator of the Quilter's Affair, says it best: "Close on the heels of July 4th celebrations, the town of Sisters, Oregon, gets ready to open its arms and explode with the excitement of a weeklong educational experience like none other. Sisters High School is where it all begins. From the minute cars pull into that parking lot, one can just feel the pull of anticipation. They will finally get to meet instructors they have only read about in magazines or heard about from friends who have attended past Quilter's Affair events. They will meet other students from around the world, and they will find creative inspiration around every corner.

"Walking through the front door, one might instantly be reminded of what it was like to start high school. Lots of tables, chairs, displays, quilts, registration areas, and so many people eager for the experience. All senses are on alert. Of course, the first order of business is to find their classroom where the magic begins. With birds singing outside, the sunshine warming their faces, and guided by high school students, one begins the trek to find just the right spot to set up for the day. The day goes fast and they don't want to miss a thing. It is a happy place filled with smiles, helping hands, and oh, so much to learn. It's not hard to feel the creativity flowing through the hallways.

"This excitement carries throughout the week with events scheduled in the evenings and learning about the quaint little town of Sisters. The environment provides a beautiful backdrop for a week filled with relaxation, inspiration, and education. All in all, it is a great place and time to rejuvenate one's creative soul."

Quilter's Affair Bingo Night

Jackie Erickson is the force behind the Quilter's Affair Bingo Night, and what a fun-filled evening it is! Hosted by two Quilter's Affair teachers and assisted by Valori and the Stitchin' Post staff and volunteers, the evening moves at a quick, electrifying pace.

We play between fifteen and twenty games, depending on time allotted. Bingo night usually fills within three days of the Quilter's Affair registration opening. The word is out, and you've got to be quick on the draw if you want to participate.

Each participant receives a small gift as they enter the high school. The winner of every game receives a fantastic prize, and all the players sitting at the winners table also receive a smaller prize. Well-known quilter Scott Hansen creates an amazing quilt every year as the prize for the final game of the evening, Blackout Bingo!

Lately, some of our staff have taken to dressing up. Currently, two unidentified pink unicorns have graced our bingo night to hand out prizes. I can't wait to see what shows up year after year. Every year we pass out more than 400 gifts and prizes. Some are large, some are small, but one thing is for sure: Everyone goes away happy and exhausted from having so much fun!

Two unidentified pink unicorns pop in for bingo night to help hand out prizes.

"Since [I moved] to Sisters in 2007, Jean has been a friend, a teacher, and an unending source of inspiration. She is supportive and always willing to help. Congratulations, Jean, for your 50 years as a local leader and legend."—Sharon Carvalho, instructor

I discovered Rosalie Dace's stunning work when I was teaching in New Zealand. Rosalie is a celebrated quilter and instructor based in Durban, South Africa. I tracked her down and found out she was coming to the States to teach, so I invited her to come to Sisters. It became an annual event, with her teaching in the store and at Quilter's Affair for more than ten years.

Rosalie shares, "I feel very privileged to have become an instructor at both the Stitchin' Post and Quilter's Affair, and I soon knew that we had the same approach to what we were doing … to educate, enrich, and enjoy. As an instructor, I was always treated professionally and with respect, but Jean always went that extra mile that showed how intensely engaged she was with developing her customers and students. While Jean has engendered a respect for the traditions from which quiltmaking comes, it was always clear that new ideas were welcome. As our world changed, she and Valori too embraced the possibilities of online shopping and classes, which has meant that I have been able to continue teaching at the Stitchin' Post via Zoom. You draw customers and students from the local community that you serve, as well [as] from far afield. I could then also enjoy how you honor local as well as national and international artists and show their work at the Stitchin' Post. We all feel we belong there, where we can learn, teach, make new discoveries and new friends."

Journeys 4: Night Flight, by Rosalie Dace.

"Coming to the Quilter's Affair and teaching was life changing for me. And meeting Jean Wells was a big part of that. I had always been very structured and symmetrical in my quilting, and seeing her work was freeing to me in a way I can't describe! Her love and reverence of the earth came alive in elements of color and fabric that I had never imagined. She has a gift for making people feel through her quilting art. But even more than that, she and Valori were kind and welcomed me with a sisterhood I hadn't before experienced. Congratulations, Jean and Valori, you are loved and admired."—Jenny Doan, founder of Missouri Star Quilting

For so many quilters, teaching at Quilter's Affair and journeying to Sisters has become an eagerly anticipated treat. "I have been quilting since I was a little girl, but it wasn't until I was in my twenties that I started exploring quiltmaking outside of my own designs and what my mother taught me. As soon as I did, I found Jean and Val's books, and they're still in my library today as firm treasures. Teaching at Quilter's Affair and exhibiting at the [Sisters] Outdoor Quilt Show was a dream for years, and I feel incredibly privileged to be invited back so often. The welcoming community, [the] atmosphere of friendship, and the staff's deep belief in the education of quilters is an experience to treasure, and the magic of this wonderful week is something I hope every quilter is able to experience at least once," shares Sarah Fielke, Australian instructor.

Lynn Koolish offers a variety of surface design workshops in the art room during Quilter's Affair.

Scott Hansen feels that "Coming to Sisters, Oregon, every summer has become my yearly mecca for a creative escape from everyday life.

"The students and fellow teachers at Quilter's Affair feel like family now, and the whole week, including the amazing show, feels like Christmas, summer camp, and [a] family reunion every year.

"I am so grateful to Jean for starting this event and to Valori for taking it forward into the future. Months before this wonderful week, I get more and more excited. I can smell the dry pine high desert and hear the chatter of quilters and humming of machines as all of [the] students and teachers gather together to create and explore quilty concepts during Quilter's Affair. And then show day! That grand display of makers' hearts and minds showing *everywhere* via a myriad of color combinations, techniques, and imaginations. Inspiring so many people, non-quilters included! I am so blessed to participate in this event. All of my other quilty and vacation plans wrap around this amazing event."

"One of the greatest nights of my life was when I was the Friday evening speaker at Quilter's Affair. It was a packed house, and I had Valori's whole family (Jean's five grandchildren and her brother, Jason) helping me unfold and show my quilts. The joy, the sparkling goodwill, the entire feeling in the room made me feel I was being lifted on clouds of positivity. The atmosphere that Jean and Valori and their staff have created makes the whole week unusually delightful."—Joe Cunningham, quilt artist

LEFT • In addition to attending classes, Quilter's Affair attendees can also attend lectures by well known quilters, such as this talk given by Joe Cunningham. Joe is discussing his quilt *The Sleeping Protestors of Kyiv*.

TOP (3) • From crazy quilting to Log Cabin blocks, attendees can find offerings covering the full spectrum of quilting.

Two of my grandchildren were born during the summer, so on a couple of occasions it was a very pregnant Valori pitching in at Quilter's Affair. Lou Shafer reminisces that "It was a pleasure to watch Valori grow through the years as well. We were always so happy to see her photographic skills honed and polished, and loved when she became more involved with Quilter's Affair. The joy of Olivia's arrival (her first daughter), the brilliant timing of Violette's arrival post-QA, by a week, and rounding out the three musketeers with her Teague! Seeing her unleash her artistic talents and share her love of Morocco with her 'Creatives Retreats' is heartwarming."

Instructor and author Laura Wasilowski notes that "It is amazing what Jean and Valori have created! [Jean], her family, the town of Sisters, and the Quilter's Affair community have given us a joyful event to celebrate each year."

When I began writing this book, I reached out to instructors who have taught at Quilter's Affair over the years and the response was simply overwhelming.

"I had the great privilege of lecturing and teaching … I was so amazed at how an entire town opened their arms to receive another town full of excited quilters. Lecturing in the hot sun with a field full of attendees was a highlight and a testament to the value this event provided."—Kaye England, designer, instructor, and author

"Valori and Jean and their team always made the presenters feel such a part of the event, and I truly enjoyed being in an atmosphere that was filled with excitement and wonder at the spectacular display of a town full of quilts. It was a memory I will cherish. Who wouldn't want to live in a Quilt Town."—Carolyn Friedlander, designer, instructor, and author

"Over the years, I've had the privilege of attending and teaching at the Sisters [Outdoor] Quilt Show. From bud to blossom, today's success is a clear testament to Jean and Val, their resilience, and unshakable dedication to Sisters and the quilting industry. The Sisters [Outdoor] Quilt Show has become a beloved tradition, fostering a sense of community and connection among quilters, and Jean's sincere and consistent commitment [have] laid the groundwork for the show's continued success. The legacy that Jean [has] built will continue to inspire future generations, ensuring that the spirit of creativity and community thrives in Sisters for years to come."—Sue Spargo, designer, instructor

LEFT • The normally sedate high school classrooms burst with color for one week in July.

RIGHT • *Truffle Duffel*, by Sue Spargo.

"Watching Jean and Val comingle their skills and talents over the past years has been nothing short of amazing." shares Karla Alexander, quilting instructor and volunteer. "People come from near and far to simply enjoy the adventures they provide in small-town USA! While we all have different dreams and goals, I can assure you, visiting Sisters and meeting Jean and Val can be found on most every quilter's bucket list. I feel delighted to say I have been lucky enough to benefit in one way or another from all they have to offer. If you haven't had this pleasure, add it to your bucket list—you won't be disappointed."

"One of my favorite places to teach is at Quilter's Affair. I find the students wonderful, the venue is fun and comfortable, and the staff and Jean are so good to us. Waking [up to] the outdoor Quilt Show after the week of workshops is inspiring and beautiful. And a trip to the quilt shop is just the icing on the delicious cake!!" shares Katie Pasquini, longtime instructor. Katie comes from a large family of quilters in Northern California. A few years ago, they all came to Sisters with their quilts, and their quilts were all hung in the show.

LEFT • Sujata Shah, featured instructor in 2024, in front of one of her special exhibit quilts in 2024.

RIGHT • Fabric art bowl in progress during a Hilde Moran class.

LEFT • Special exhibit quilts by featured instructor Jennifer Sampou.

MIDDLE AND RIGHT • The Teacher's Pavillion is always a big draw. In addition to containing some amazing work, the park location allows visitors a respite from the concrete sidewalks.

"I came to know of Jean in 2002 when I was working at my local quilt shop. Through her books, I admired her personal style of quilting ... based on inspirations from nature. The impact Jean has on the quilters, teachers, and for community building through Sisters Outdoor Quilt Show and Quilter's Affair is immeasurable. Creating a gathering place that brings people together from all over the country and the world is quite an achievement. Her encouragement and passion have made a lasting impression and inspired me to follow my own path in quilting and teaching.

"I look forward to the Sisters Outdoor Quilt Show each year as I looked forward to the Festival of Colors during my childhood in India."—Sujata Shah, instructor

"One of the things I most admire and appreciate about Jean, is how she supports and promotes those of us in the quilting industry. When I was just beginning to teach, Jean invited me to teach at the Stitchin' Post and introduced me to the wonderful place that is Sisters and to the amazing Stitchin' Post store. And she (and Valori) continue to provide a supportive venue there for so many teachers and students.

"Jean also encouraged me to talk to Valori about teaching at Quilter's Affair, and it has become my absolute favorite place to teach. Valori and Jean have created such a creative and nurturing environment. Teachers and students love coming to Sisters for the week—for the classes as well as the [Sisters] Outdoor Quilt Show. As a teacher, I feel totally appreciated and supported—thank you, Val and Jean!"—Lynn Koolish, instructor and editor

Sisters, Oregon—Five Decades of Quilting in America

"Sisters Outdoor Quilt Show has been one of my favorite events to participate in for many years. There is an amazing creative energy that is supported by the eclectic group of high-end quilt artists, set in the most beautiful natural setting. The quilts absolutely glow in the morning sun as the finale to another year of artistic expression through our love of textiles."—Rob Appell

The Quilter's Affair isn't the only education opportunity Sisters has to offer. Beyond individual classes, Sisters welcomes artists in residence, who come to absorb the local environment and art, and learn from other masters. Giuseppe Ribaudo of Giucy Giuce, instructor and the 2024 artist in residence, shares his thoughts on the experience. "It's just after midnight on a moonless night. A field of stars stretches infinitely beyond the Three Sisters mountains, their snow-covered tops agleam in the starlight. Shaking the cold from my body as I enter the studio, the pungent scent of juniper still hangs in the air. I poke at the fire. Listless little flames lurch back to life as I throw another log into the stove.

"When these mountains came into view as I drove into Sisters for the first time, I knew there was magic here. I remember basking in their magnificence from Jean Wells's backyard. In her studio, I spied treasures everywhere. Trinkets and recollections strewn amongst her fabric and masterfully crafted projects. Looking out the window at the mountains, I thought, 'Wow, what an incredible place to get to create.'"

"It has been a couple of years since that first visit to Sisters. I write this from my studio at Pine Meadow Ranch, where I'm taking part in my first artist's residency. For one month, I get to make believe I live in this wonderful town. The

LEFT • Quilts by Giuseppe Ribaudo of Giucy Giuce displayed at the Save It for Sunday! event.

RIGHT • More of Giuseppe's quilts on display at FivePine Lodge.

Sisters, Oregon—Five Decades of Quilting in America

last two weeks, I have been working on a special project for the upcoming Quilter's Affair. Surrounded by pieces in various stages of doneness, that same magic that wrapped me in a spell on my first day still has its power over me.

"I like to imagine Jean sensed that same magic when she first hung quilts outside her shop 50 years ago. For me, and for many, this event has become a pivotal moment of the year. It's much more than just coming together to take classes and see quilts. The town vibrates when its streets are filled with colorful quilts fluttering in the gentle breeze. You can sense this collective energy. It's in and around every one of us who are lucky enough to wander the sun-soaked streets on the second Saturday in July.

"Writing this, I keep returning to that moment in Jean's studio where I marveled at getting to work with the mountains just a stone's throw from my window. I was getting to take in the Three Sisters every day while I stitched my own story? Magic. I'm telling you. It defies any other explanation."

local Artists

Greetings From Sisters *mural by Katie Daisy and Karen Eland.*

Quilts aren't just confined to clotheslines, they can sometimes also be found on and around other public art. This statue was in front of Leavitt's Western Wear for years.

Quilting is, by far, not the only art form that flourishes in Sisters. With such an awe-inspiring natural setting, it's no wonder that painters, sculptors, poets, authors, and many more artists gravitate toward this art-friendly small town. Artists thrive on inspiration, and that flows back and forth between the various disciplines present in Sisters. You'll find quilts and quilt inspiration peeking through paintings and in sculpture, painterly influences in quilts, and so much more confluence of themes and disciplines.

When young graphic artist, Dennis McGregor, moved to town he suggested creating a painting to be used as a poster for the Quilt Show. At the time, a small group of women and I were putting on the show, and we'd had Marina Wood, a local illustrator, create a poster a few years before. When Dennis approached me and told me the cost, I could see it would be a financial risk, and I would need to save up the funds to pay him and the printing costs. But it worked! Having a gorgeous color poster by a local artist was just the beginning of a beautiful part of the annual show.

This relationship continued and Dennis's posters are now collector's items. They have inspired other art that you see in boutiques and galleries throughout town. In part, Dennis helped Sisters become a mecca for artists. As evidence to the ties that bind various artists and art forms together in this special place, in 2015, Dennis McGregor wrote a song about the quilt show. He performed the song, accompanied by Brad Tisdale from the folk festival, at our fundraiser and 40th anniversary celebration.

40th Anniversary Song
by Dennis McGregor and Brad Tisdale

I came to this place back in '89
It was July, summertime,
Bought a little house on the edge of town
Moved right in, took a look around
Right away I saw something strange
As I looked toward the mountain range
There were all kinds of colors flapping in the breeze
Between the buildings and the trees
I didn't know what it was all about
So I walked down the road to find out
What I saw was a big surprise
I could not believe my eyes ...
It was blankets! The handmade kind
Everywhere a blanket hangin' from a line ...
This brought questions to my mind
And the person in charge wasn't hard to find
She stood right out from the crowd
Said to me right out loud
First of all, if you want to get along
You're gonna have to stop saying it wrong
The word's not blanket, the word is quilt!!
Q—U—I—L—T!
I apologized but I couldn't resist
To ask about the pincushion on her wrist
And the thimbles on her fingers with needles between
She offered her hand saying, 'My name's Jean Wells, that is,
W—E—with double L's',
That is how I met Jean Wells!
Jean Wells! Jean Wells! Jean Wells! Jean Wells!
Jean, Jean, Quilt Show queen
Busiest woman I ever seen,
She had kids and a cat and a new husband
Dog and a garden and fabric store
With employees and inventory
Bills to pay and so much more,
Quilts to make and books to write
I wonder if she sleeps at night ... ?
Jean Wells! Jean Wells! Jean Wells! Jean Wells!
Next thing you know, another year went by
And volunteer firefighters were hangin' 'em high
From the highway, folks were gawking
Parked their cars, started walking
Quilt to quilt, street to street
Buying souvenirs and food to eat
Hotels full and gas pumps pumping
Man, she really started something!
Makes this town look like a rainbow
Once a year, with her quilt show
She's done it now for 40 years,
So let's fill this room with cheers ...
Jean Wells! Jean Wells! Jean Wells! Jean Wells!

Helen G. Schmidling of the Sisters Arts Association gives a little more background. "[The] Sisters Arts Association (SAA) was founded in 2015 by artists and supporters who believe that the arts are an important part of a healthy community, enriching culture and contributing to a strong and resilient economy. SAA supports and promotes the work of individual artists, artist studios, art galleries, makers collectives and studios, a theater company, and art-friendly businesses.

TOP • Sculpture by Selena Jones. Left to right, Valori, Selena, me, and Ana Varas.

LEFT • Visitors enjoy art by other local artists as they meander through town admiring the quilts.

RIGHT • Sign spotted at C&C Nursery in town. Quilting has spread tendrils throughout town.

"Yearlong events coordinated and sponsored by SAA include a monthly Fourth Friday Artwalk through the Galleries of Sisters, an annual Artist Studio Tour, art instruction and demonstrations, live talks and performances and networking opportunities."

The current Executive Director, Dawn M. Boyd points out that "While the Quilt Show focuses on celebrating quilts, we have loved our partnership with Central Oregon artists for our show posters over the years. We have also had the lovely opportunity to share additional art mediums throughout the years. Gallery showings inside of the Stitchin' Post might feature local guild or individual quilter exhibits, stained glass art, and fiber art works, all made by local artisans."

LEFT • Humans aren't the only fans of the Sisters Outdoor Quilt Show. As the largest outdoor quilt show in the world, it is one of the only shows to allow dogs, and the occassional wildlife, in to take in the show.

MIDDLE • Serendipity sometimes plays a hand in crafting a quilt display!

RIGHT • *The Decade Quilt* by Ginn Staines (left) and *City Sampler at Night* by Emily Armstrong (right).

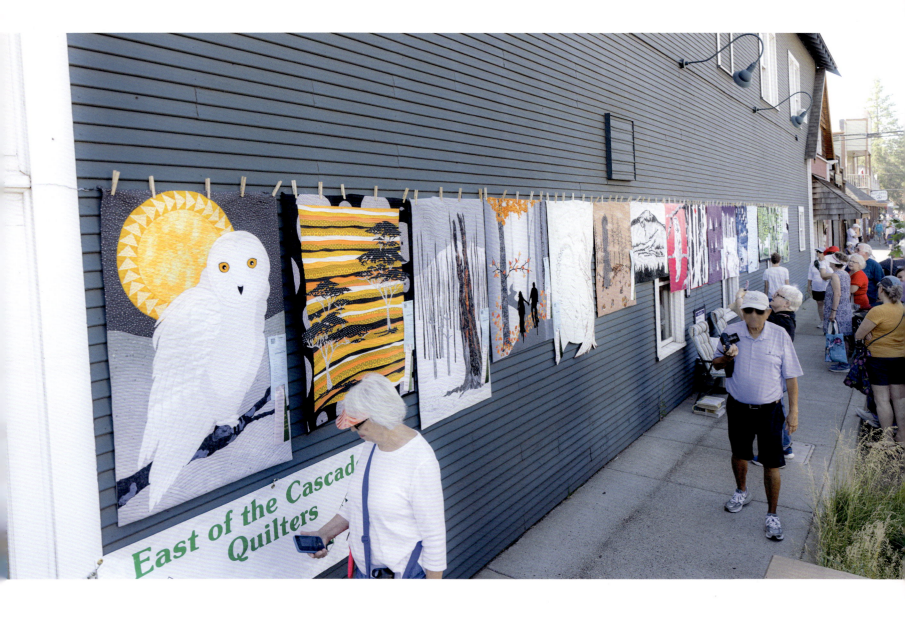

"The Sisters Quilt show brings community members and businesses together in a celebration of the arts. The focus is on quilts, but the subject matter covers the whole of art history, from traditional folk arts to contemporary themes and styles. I have always been impressed by the time, energy, skills, and thinking that go into the making of so many of the quilts I've seen over the last 34 years I have lived in Sisters. It is a celebration of the love of working with one's hands and heart," shares Paul Alan Bennett, printmaker, painter, and poster artist.

Special exhibit by the East of the Cascades Quilters guild of Sisters, showcasing their challenge quilts. The 2024 theme being black, white, and one color.

The WISH Card Program

In 2007, the tiniest of quilts inspired a momentous project, Wish Upon a Card. Those weren't actually quilts—they were fabric postcards that launched this popular Quilt Show endeavor.

As with many Quilt Show pursuits, we partnered with a local organization—in this case, Wendy's Wish Foundation—to share the proceeds from the auction and sale of the donated postcards. Wendy's Wish provided funding for nonmedical expenses for people undergoing cancer treatment.

Wendy, who had recently passed away from cancer, was a quilter, and her husband and friends were eager to participate in and support the project. The Wendy's Wish Foundation later disbanded, so the WISH Project funds now support the Sisters Outdoor Quilt Show Scholarship fund and the show.

Other local artisans participate in the program, like Myrna Dow of High Desert Frameworks. Myrna says, "The Wish Upon a Card project is very dear to my heart. It is a celebration of small things quilted. When I saw the beautiful fabric postcards, I realized it was an opportunity to give back to an organization that has been so important to the Sisters community. Over the years, we framed over 900 fabric postcards and raised more than $150,000 in support of people [who] struggled with cancer, students blossoming out into new careers and the fabulous Sisters Outdoor Quilt Show. I was honored to work with the Quilt Show and the incredible Quilter's Affair teachers, plus a community of quilters worldwide, to showcase their artwork and raise money for such a worthy cause."

Robyn Gold took over management of the program in 2021. "In 2023, we received more than 500 cards, including 56 cards from Germany," Robin says. "These cards in particular indicate the far reach of the Quilt Show: The German ladies who participated found out about the show from an Instagram post. We also receive cards from across the United States and Canada.

"Over the time I've been coordinating the WISH Card program, I have learned that it truly does take a village to put on the Quilt Show. It takes a team of sixteen of us just to manage the ... program! It has been, and will continue to be, a wonderful opportunity to become involved in the community and to give back to our community, while having a great amount of fun. How many people get to actively participate in an activity considered by many quilters to be a bucket-list item?! We're lucky!"

Framed teacher WISH card created and donated by Jean Wells.

In 2009, a group in Bend put on the Broadway musical *Quilters*. Quilters from Sisters and Bend created all of the quilts that were used as props, some of which were sold as a fundraiser for the Sisters Outdoor Quilt Show.

"I worked with Valori in North Carolina on her very first line of fabric in 1998, titled Shades of Serenity, and it remains one of my favorite collections. Over the years, she has evolved as an artist. I have watched Val grow and succeed as an artist, [a] daughter, a shop owner, an author, a traveler, a friend, and a mother. She is an amazing individual who empowers herself and others along her journey. Her talent, her ideas, her kindness, her grace, and her strength are just a few of the many attributes that make her such an amazing and inspiring force. Her work 25 years later continues to push the limits, to impress, to be relevant, and to inspire makers around the world! It is an honor and a privilege to know Valori Wells and to call her my friend."—Debbie Driscoll Stark, *Creative Director for FreeSpirit Fabrics*

Kathy Deggendorfer has been a supporter of the Quilt Show since she moved to Sisters in 1994. "I grew up in a little town outside Portland, Oregon. We didn't watch much TV, but because my mom was an art major in college, our house was always full of materials for creating ... pens, pencils, paper, and paint. My mom was a genius when it came to sewing, but that talent didn't pass on to me ... I just loved looking at the fabrics and prints in her stash. Sewing wasn't my thing but I always had a pencil or a paintbrush in my hand.

"My husband and I met going to university in Italy, and after we married in 1973, we moved to Bend. We moved to Sisters when our daughter entered high school in 1994. I built myself a studio in our barn and began to create colorful watercolors that reflected my view of the mountains and pine forests that surround Sisters. With help from a local art gallery, I

discovered that my work resonated with others and began to paint professionally.

"Over the years, I have designed several fabric lines for the quilting market and done licensed product design for Columbia Sportswear. In the last ten years, I have worked with a local tile manufacturer to create colorful tile murals. Working with tile allows me to have public art installations in hospitals, colleges, public parks, and even the Federal Reserve Bank of San Francisco.

"One of my proudest accomplishments is to have created the poster for the Sisters Outdoor Quilt Show five times! Nothing is more fun than to work with the generous and creative people who run and attend the Sisters Outdoor Quilt Show.

LEFT • All three quilts feature Valori Wells's Grace line of fabric from 2024. The designs are created from hand-carved designs and block printed on fabric.

MIDDLE • Valori, in front of her inspiration wall.

RIGHT • Valori, deep in her process of block printing.

"I continue to paint professionally, but much of my time now is devoted to working with the Roundhouse Foundation. I founded the organization in 2002 to support arts and culture in the Central Oregon area. Today we have a much larger footprint but still focus on looking for creative solutions to unique problems in rural communities. We own and operate Pine Meadow Ranch just outside of Sisters where we host a thriving artist residency program and practice regenerative agriculture on our farm lands." Kathy is the poster artist for 2025.

TOP • Whisper Quilt Project quilts from Central Oregon Studio Art Quilt Associates members. They are displayed on the round barn at the Pine Meadow Ranch.

RIGHT • Official 2025 poster, *Mountain Meadow*, by Kathy Deggendorfer.

I met local quilter Colleen Blackwood in the early days of opening the store. She went on to become an instructor for Quilter's Affair and volunteers as a team leader for hanging quilts on Quilt Show day. "Quilt Show day was a family and community event. Husbands were enlisted to assist in the hanging of quilts. Business owners brought ladders, new friends were made and old friends were greeted with smiles and full hearts. The crowds of quilters wandered through all the quilts displayed, smiling with approval of efforts by others. Some took the time to read about the maker and the quilt; others just enjoyed the colors and patterns from the middle of the road. Prior to cell phones and walkie-talkies, if the wind blew a quilt out of its clothes pins, we would grab a chair or bench and enlist those passing by to help us hang it back up for all to enjoy.

"I have been so blessed to meet and become friends with amazing, caring, creative women during the week of Quilter's Affair classes prior to the Quilt Show. The teachers I learned from are a list of important quilters of this era ... each of them added to my quilting heritage and future in their own way. The students who travel from around the globe to attend the classes and show are their own reward in the field of inspiration and true friendship. It is like an annual reunion of like-minded creative, wonderful people [who] I look forward to seeing every year."

We Stitch

By Colleen Blackwood

We stitch, joining us to others
At the heart,
Together
Our stitches form a bond
That makes us stronger
A family of friends stitch
Themselves stronger with
Needle and thread.
Our stitches become a life rope,
A safety net,
Silent signals of sisterhood
Stitched in place by hands
Held together by spirits
Gently guiding the needles
As we stitch.

the Show Today

The sun is just peeking over the buildings as Sisters prepares to welcome thousands of visitors. Shop owner Casey Boyd adds to the ambiance of the day by lending her truck to the displays. Marsh Song *by Martha Phair Sanders is hung on a quilt stand in this vintage truck on Quilt Show day.*

The Quilt Show may have more than 1,000 quilts hung in 2025, but the small town feeling still exists as if it were 1975. It is truly still a day of sharing. The logging trucks driving through town are gone, but our little town is full of independent retailers, art galleries, practicing artists, and outdoor recreation.

LEFT • Starting the day by watching volunteer firefighters hang quilts on the side of the shop is a time-tested tradition. This very first quilt to go up was *Birds of a Feather* by Nancy Hamilton.

RIGHT • Veteran visitors know to be sure to stroll up and down each street so they don't miss a thing.

The quilts are varied, from an antique treasure, to a modern version of log cabin, to a landscape, to the first quilt made by a new quilter. New friendships are kindled and old friends gather once a year. The magic exists today just as it did that second Saturday in July in 1975 when twelve family quilts were displayed.

LEFT • *Typographic Circle*, by Emily Cier offers readers a chance to get in close and explore the detail.

MIDDLE • Aimee Hobson showed her very first quilt in the 2024 show. She then gifted it to her mother, Sheila Schweizer, for her birthday. A true celebration about why we quilt!

RIGHT • Cool grass, a little shade, and a lot of color greet those who come to explore the Teacher's Pavilion.

Save It for Sunday!

As the Quilt Show has always been looking to expand its celebration of art, skill, and heritage of quilting and fiber arts, it seemed very natural to expand the celebration beyond the single Quilt Show day. In 2013, a new tradition was added—Save It for Sunday!

TOP • More of my quilts hung for the Save It for Sunday event.

BOTTOM LEFT • *Firefly*, by Jean Wells hung at FivePine Lodge for Save It for Sunday!

BOTTOM MIDDLE • *Flower Pop*, by Jenny Pedigo and Helen Robinson.

RIGHT • Rich MacConnell and Becca hanging one of Sarah Fielke's quilts in anticipation of the first visitors Sunday morning.

Collaborating with our beautiful FivePine Lodge & Conference Center, the show invites a guest artist and Quilter's Affair instructor to share their own stories and quilts in a more intimate setting. The quilts are hung among the pines throughout the walking path and along the creek that winds through the FivePine Lodge campus. The guest artist leads small groups through their quilt story path, enjoying the quietness and intimacy of this idyllic setting.

In between the two walking tours, the guest artist is given the chance to speak to a larger group of quilt aficionados, sharing their journey as a quilter, designer, and artist.

Our Save It for Sunday! event is an opportunity for quilters to savor all that the Sisters quilting community has to offer, ending their time with us in a setting that perfectly epitomizes my vision from so many years ago—celebrating, educating, and encouraging each one of us in our quilting journey.

Save It for Sunday! reiterates what is special about this place, these people, and this show. It allows for more interconnectedness with the featured artists. Quilters leave with a sense of serenity that energizes them to go home and create.

TOP AND RIGHT • Quilts shared by Carolyn Friedlander during her Save It for Sunday! exhibit.

"Thirty years ago, my wife Zoe and I walked the Quilt Show for the first time. We were taken by the artists' expressions of color, design, and craftsmanship. We recognized that these artists dreamed of their quilts and then quilted their dreams. It takes courage to be an artist. We were seeing unique expressions of self.

"What I didn't understand was that quilting is contagious. That one day soon my wife would have a studio, a longarm, and baskets filled with amazing fabric. That, over the years, she would create many treasured quilts for our family and closest friends. And in her studio she would create a quiet place to find her artist self.

"None of this would have happened without the love and friendship of the Wells family."—William Willitts, *the visionary mind behind the FivePine campus*

LEFT • *Jewels*, hung as part of Valori's Save It for Sunday!

RIGHT (4) • My daughter, Valori's quilts hung for her exhibit.

At first light, before the bustle of show day begins, I pause to think of all of the family and quilting friends who are no longer with us.

Quilting in Sisters, Oregon, is like a three-ring circus with The Stitchin' Post all decked out in fabric and quilts, the Quilter's Affair welcoming 1,200 students and 30 instructors, and the Sisters Outdoor Quilt Show preparing to welcome thousands of folks to our small town to join in the celebration of the creative quilting experience.

To me, in the end, it all comes down to a special day of sharing, with so many people, the joy found in being a creative person. Each year it warms my heart to see all the special moments unfold throughout the day; from a quilter bringing her whole family to see her first quilt on display; a child seeing their very own quilt hanging in the show; or a daughter making her first quilt, entering it in the show, and then gifting it on the spot to her mother. Quilting has no boundaries. Right alongside those new quilters, I see famous quilters showing their quilts in an outdoor setting, standing proudly with big grins and explaining to a complete novice how they created them. My happiness is bringing together all aspects of this artform we love and you'll find special exhibits like QuiltCon winners hung alongside antique family quilts.

It's gratifying to see how much the show has brought to my community and humbling to witness how much my town, neighbors, and family members have embraced the show. From interactions with residents, business owners, firefighters, and sheriff's deputies, attendees always comment on how welcoming our community is. Nowhere else would we have gotten such enthusiastic participation from the fire and sheriff's departments. One of the deputies told me he always tries to be assigned the crosswalk by the Stitchin' Post, which feels like the greatest compliment.

After all these years, I still rise at 5:30 am, come to town by 6:00 am, and take a deep breath, remembering the special quilting friends and family members we have lost. Then the day begins and I get the shivers as I watch one quilt hung after another until our special little town is draped in color. Whether this is your first visit, your 50th, or just on your bucket list, you are welcome and I hope you get to experience a little bit of our magic.

Like all good things, the sun eventually sets on each day of quilting in Sisters. Two of Valori's quilts flank one of mine. In the background you can see donkey Juanita looking on.

177
The Show Today

THE Sisters OUTDOOR QUILT SHOW Posters

1989
Marina Wood
The first official poster.

1992
Dennis McGregor
Whirlwind.

1993
Dennis McGregor
Quilt Show.

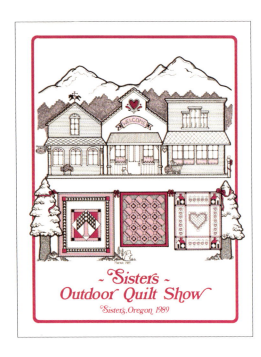
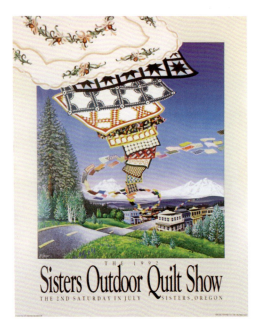
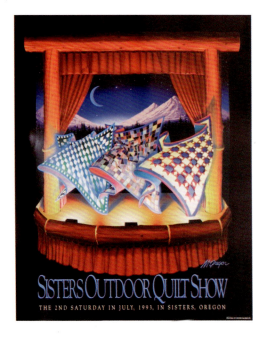

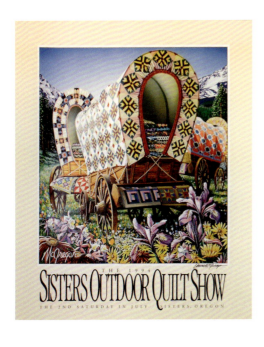
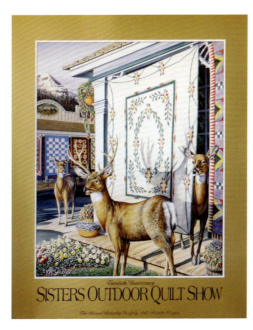

1994
Dennis McGregor
Oregon Trail.

1995
Dennis McGregor
Locals. *Sisters, situated next to a national forest, has town deer that stroll around in the early mornings and evenings.*

1996
Dennis McGregor
Sunflowers.

1997
Dennis McGregor
Log Cabin Settlers.

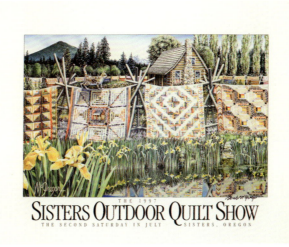

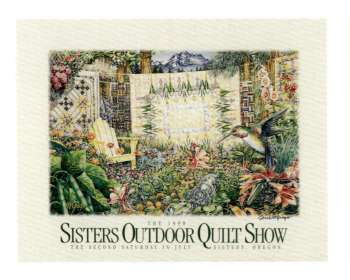
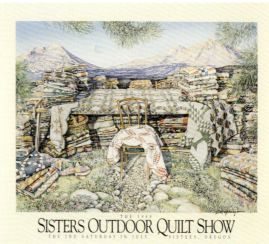
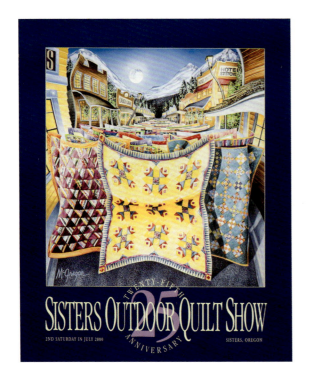

1998
Dennis McGregor
McGregor's Garden.

1999
Dennis McGregor
Cascade of Quilts.

2000
Dennis McGregor
Parade. *What better way to celebrate an anniversary than a quilted parade!*

2001
Dennis McGregor
Nine Patch Horse.

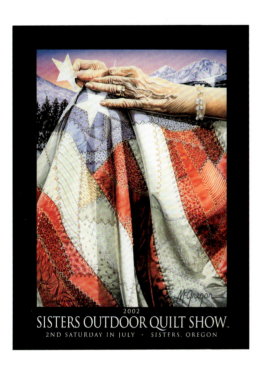
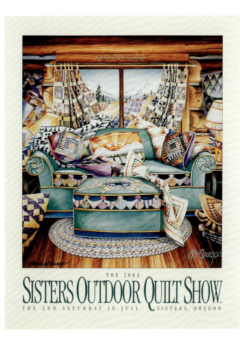

2002
Dennis McGregor
Patriot's Needle.

2003
Dennis McGregor
Lodge.

2004
Dennis McGregor
Campfire Quilts.

2005
Dennis McGregor
Hands All Around the World
Coming Together in Quilting.

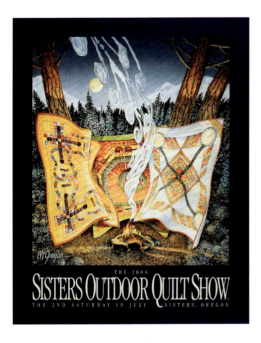
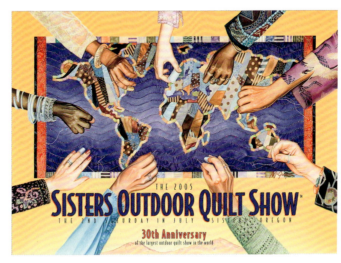

The Sisters Outdoor Quilt Show Posters

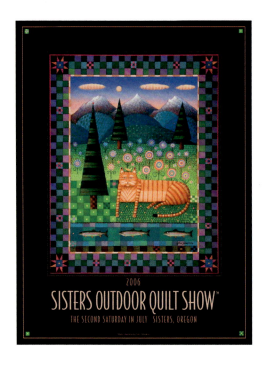
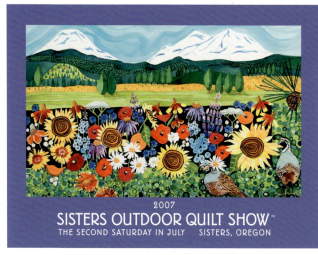
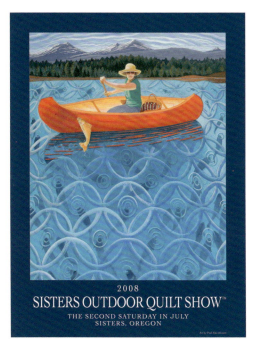

2006
John Simpkins
Mystic Meadow.

2007
Kathy Deggendorfer
Nature's Inspiration.

2008
Paul Alan Bennett
Wedding Ring Blues.

2009
Dan Rickards
Summer Bliss.

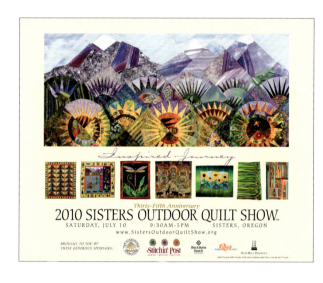

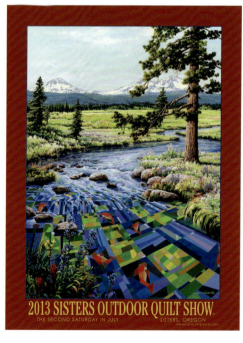

2010
Quilts by Jean Wells.
Inspired Journey. *To celebrate the 35th anniversary of the Quilt Show, several of my quilts were featured on the show poster, showcasing my journey in quiltmaking and design.*

2011
Kathy Deggendorfer
Nature's Symphony.

2012
Kathy Deggendorfer
Go to Town.

2013
Dan Rickards
Streams of Color.

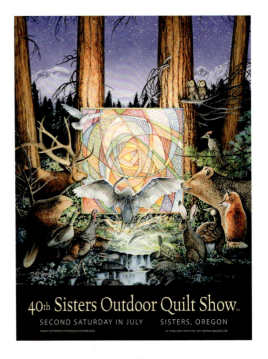
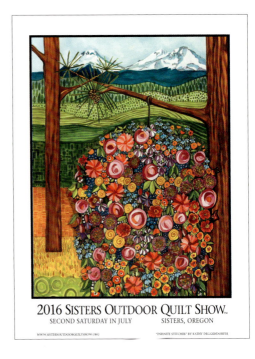
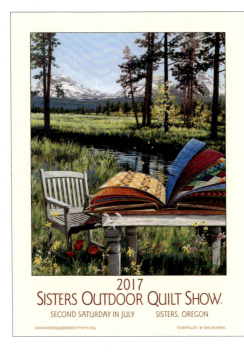

2014
Dan Rickards
It Takes a Village.

2015
Dennis McGregor
A Timeless Tapestry.

2016
Kathy Deggendorfer
Infinite Stitches.

2017
Dan Rickards
Storytellers.

Sisters, Oregon—Five Decades of Quilting in America

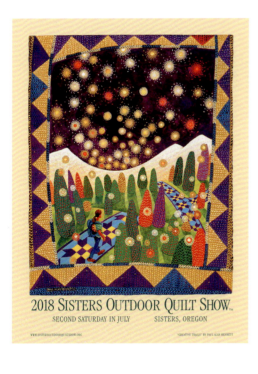
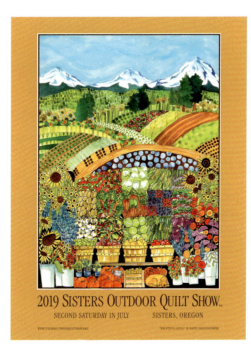

2018
Paul Alan Bennett
Creative Trails.

2019
Kathy Deggendorfer
Bountiful Living.

2020
Dan Rickards
My Kind of Town.

2021
Donna Rice
Renewal.

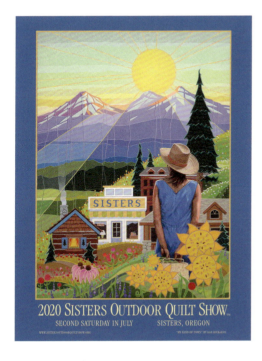

The Sisters Outdoor Quilt Show Posters

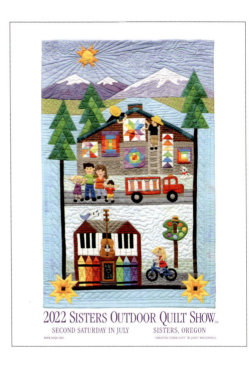
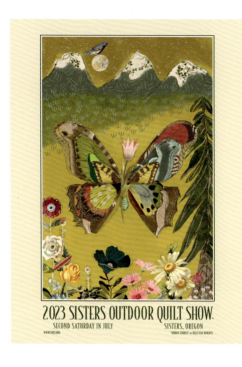

2022
Janet MacConnell
Creating Community.

2023
Kelly Ray Roberts
Hidden Stories.

2024
Cheryl Chapman
Dreamscapes.

2025
Kathy Deggendorfer
Mountain Meadow.

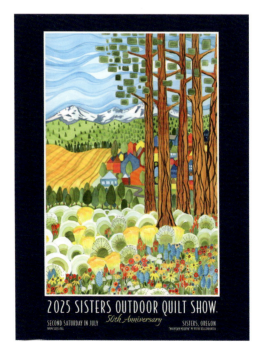

PHOTOGRAPHY CREDITS

Andrew Penniman
Pages 81, 86, 87.

Chloe Frazee
Page 192.

Dawn M. Boyd
Pages 58 (left), 62 (bottom right).

Gary Alvis
Pages 38–41, 44, 47, 50, 52, 56 (top), 57, 61 (bottom left and right), 64 (left), 67, 69 (bottom), 75 (left and bottom right), 77 (left), 78, 84, 88, 93, 103, 105, 178 (center and right), 179, 180, 181, 182 (top left, bottom right), 183 (top left and bottom right), 184 (top left and right, bottom right), 185 (bottom left and right), 186 (top left and right, bottom left).

Jean Wells
Pages 13, 15, 17 (bottom), 18, 21, 22, 24 (bottom), 25, 26, 27, 30, 37, 102, 109, 120, 128 (left), 138, 143, 152, 154 (bottom), 155.

June Jaeger
Pages 20, 42.

Olivia Kennedy
Back cover (bottom left), pages 9 (right), 16, 17 (top), 19, 23, 29 (left), 31, 32, 33, 35, 43, 60, 66, 69 (top), 70 (right), 71, 96 (top), 101 (right), 110, 115, 119 (bottom), 121, 122, 124, 127, 129, 131, 132, 133, 134, 135, 136, 137, 139 (right), 141, 145, 154 (top), 156 (left), 158, 161 (left), 165, 168 (right), 169.

Paige Vitek
Pages 46, 119 (top right).

Ross Chandler
Page 28.

Spencer Giles
Pages 98 (right), 126 (bottom), 146 (right), 191.

Susan Hale
Page 159.

Valori Wells
Front cover, back cover (top, bottom right), pages 5, 7, 9 (top left, bottom left), 10, 11, 12, 24 (top), 29 (right), 45, 48, 49, 51, 55, 58 (right), 59, 61 (top), 62 (top and bottom left), 63, 68, 70 (left), 72 (top), 74, 75 (top right), 79, 83, 85, 89, 90, 91, 92, 95, 96 (bottom), 97, 98 (left), 99, 100, 101 (left), 104, 105, 106, 108, 111–113, 117, 118, 119 (top left), 123, 125, 126 (top), 128 (right), 139 (left), 140, 142, 144, 146 (left), 147–149, 151, 153, 156 (right), 157, 160, 161 (right), 162, 166, 167, 168 (left), 170–177, 188, 189.

About the Author

Jean Wells is a fifth-generation Central Oregonian who has lived in Sisters, Oregon, since 1974. She opened The Stitchin' Post, one of the first quilt shops in America, after cashing in her teacher's retirement fund in 1975. Loving to sew and discovering patchwork led her to a lifelong career as a business owner and quilting educator. For decades Jean has shared her quilted artwork and knowledge with quilters across the globe. Being the founder and creative force behind the Sisters Outdoor Quilt Show came easily to Jean as she involved herself in her community. She has won numerous awards including Citizen of the Year and Business of the Year in Sisters, Oregon, being inducted into the Quilting Hall of Fame, the Michael Kile Award, and the Deschutes County Cultural Coalition Award for working tirelessly to forward the cause and development of the arts and culture in Central Oregon.

Jean continues to create one-of-a-kind quilts and enter them in shows, winning ribbons, and participating in gallery shows. Her love of sharing ideas and techniques in the classroom drives her creatively online, in the classroom, and helping to guide the quilt show. She lives in Sisters, Oregon, with her husband, John.

Visit **jeanwellsquilts.com** online!

LEFT • *Jean's Log Cabin*, by Jean Wells

About the Contributors

It takes a village to create a book and our team put our heads together to create *Sisters, Oregon—Five Decades of Quilting in America*.

Valori Wells

Growing up at The Stitchin' Post, Valori could count the change in the cash register at five years old. She discovered photography in junior high and pursued it at the Pacific Northwest College of Art in Portland, Oregon, where she also became interested in printmaking. She soon found a career in fabric design and still designs fabric to this day. In her twenties, she took an interest in The Stitchin' Post and the rest is history. Valori now manages the store, our online business, and heads up the ever-popular Quilter's Affair event the week preceding the Quilt Show. She and Kelly Sheets lead the Creative Retreats to Morocco and Bali.

Dawn M. Boyd

Dawn M. Boyd has been the Executive Director of the Sisters Outdoor Quilt Show since January 2019, combining her passion for volunteer events coordination and organizational leadership. In this role, she guides SOQS into the future while always honoring its roots and mission. She has truly enjoyed connecting with the quilters, donors, and volunteers in the SOQS family. She takes time to pursue quilting and craft ideas in her free time. Once her five daughters began their own careers she earned a degree in Management and Organizational Leadership from George Fox University.

Olivia Kennedy

Olivia discovered the magic of photography while in high school where she attended sports events and documented them in *The Nugget Newspaper*. She also found joy in taking senior portraits. Being Valori's daughter, she has also worked at The Stitchin' Post. Post graduation, she is pursuing a career in photography.